Acknowledgments

First off, I would like to thank God for all the inspiration, dedication, and blessings He gave me in order for this book to be possible.

A very special thanks goes out to the Childs family for being so very supportive and encouraging to me. Without their prayers and love I may have never found my purpose in life.

For editing, Danny Cantrell and for artwork, Ralph Saldivar, AKA 'Cheetoz'.

Thanks to my sister, Bonnie, whom I believe my passion for cooking comes from. I love you, sis!

Thanks also to all the countless inmates who have shared time, experience, and recipes with me. Your help does not go without notice. There are just too many to list by name. These recipes are basically coast to coast; Baltimore, Colorado, Iowa, and Texas.

Last, but not least, let me say thank you to all of those individuals that helped with editing, typing, and the copying of this book. All of your time and expertise is so greatly appreciated.

All of you have truly helped a dream come true!

Taste and see that the Lord is good. How happy is the man who takes refuge in Him! Psalm 34:8.

I

About The Hookups

I have been on both sides of the fence. I have often been asked what it was like and what did we eat. I have loved to cook and bake since I was a child and have received many compliments, so I decided several years ago, to put it all on paper, and to share with everyone. You will simply be amazed at what a few simple ingredients will produce. Once you have read my book, you will never look at cookies or Ramen noodles the same again.

Not all meals are good on the inside. This is why some good ole' recipes are needed. Cellblock cooking sure beats the chow hall. Now for all of you outsiders, who love them Ramen noodles, wait until you add a couple chips and things and end up with a pizza, or even a full meal. You will simply be amazed at what you will discover within these pages.

There really is no end to what you will find as you flip through these pages. You can be sure of one thing; a stove and refrigerator will not be needed. All the recipes are no-bake, nor do any need to be refrigerated. So, for all the college students and curious people in the free world, go ahead and unhook the stove and unplug the microwave. You will not need either for these recipes.

In closing, I thank you for purchasing this book and for your support. Do not be afraid to substitute ingredients or to be creative. I truly hope and pray that each person that follows all the enclosed instructions enjoys what is produced, as much as I liked and enjoyed producing it.

Sincerely, Troy Neal Traylor, Sr.

You Can Do It!

Cellblock Cookin is a recipe book for anyone that has a desire to create a dish or sweet that leaves you craving for more. I have been around a lot of people in my time, and the biggest stumbling block I hear is the expression, "I can't", or "I wish I could." Well, you can!

The very first thing you will need to change is the way you think. It might sound difficult, but it is not as hard as one thinks.

If you have the desire, the information in this book will teach you how to cook and to create like a pro.

Practice makes perfect in life and is also the secret to self-instruction, and you will soon be a natural. If you are an experienced cook, you should be able to verify what you've practiced all along, and may even reach better results than you've ever had before.

With dedication and lots of practice, you can become among the best. It might take some time, so do not worry. You will be inspired by what you see and learn. This is a book to grow with, and growth will be achieved with regular practice and determination.

Jump right in and get right to it. You can do it, and the proof is in the pages, and of course the pudding, at the end of this book.

Have Fun!

Why Crave When You Can Create?

Are you ready to be the talk of your unit or neighborhood and discover your creative side at the same time? Well, you can, and it is both easy and fun. Imagine making both delicious and impressive looking cakes, pies, spreads, drinks, snacks, and dips that require nothing but a hot pot, spoon, bowl, and patience. No oven or refrigerator will be need! These recipes take you back to the free world and have both you and others crave for more.

Here are over 200 exciting and fun ways for you to create whatever your craving for the day might be. Maybe you are on the outside just wondering about those of us on the inside: What do they eat? What do they drink? What do they snack on? Well, here it is. You do not have to do the time, but you can learn how we dine. No matter what your reason is for purchasing this book, it is not a mistake.

Sound good so far? If so, you my friend have purchased the right book. In these pages, there are new ways and new ideas that you and your friends will truly enjoy. No meal will ever be the save! All these recipes are easy to follow as well as creative. Whether you are an experienced cook, or new to this, it does not matter. There is a new taste on every page. You must never have doubt again! Do you say, "I can't" or "I wish I could!" Well, you can! Have yourself some fun and enjoy some good ole "Cellblock Cookin."

Now chew on this. I have a very dear friend who helped me create this book. He told me that if I obeyed as well as followed his instructions, that nothing would be impossible for me. Thank you, Jesus, my friend!

Supplies Needed Inside/Outside

Spread bowls/large mixing bowls

Coffee cup/regular coffee mug/spoon/tablespoon

Hot pot/close to instant coffee pot/hot pot insert cup/12 ounce plastic cup

Empty peanut butter jar/same

Chip bags (small/large)/same

Newspaper/old newspapers

Cream cookie trays/3 row trays (Oreo)

Trash bags (small & large)/clear, plastic, trash liners

ID card/knife

Desire/same

Patience/same

Passion/same

Appetite

Helpful Hints: Almost all of these recipes require a liquid of some sort to prepare. It is better if you begin with small amounts of the suggested liquid and slowly add as you go along. This is especially true in the preparation of all the "sweets".

It is also helpful to know that dry times will vary, depending on where you are, and the time of year. Name brands might also affect dry time. A cheaper brand usually takes longer.

When you are cooking in your hot pot, the best bags to use are rice bags. Chip bags tend to separate because of the heat and can flood your food. If you use chip bags, double and triple, while cooking. Finally, do not be afraid to add or subtract from these recipes. Each person has different tastes.

Table of Contents

Protein Drink

Ingredients: 1/3 (3.2 oz) pkg instant milk
¾ cup hot water
1 heaping tbsp peanut butter
1 (43 gm) pkg instant oatmeal (any flavor)

Directions: Use an insert cup and combine instant milk and the hot water and mix well. Now stir in peanut butter until completely melted. Stir in instant oatmeal pkg and drink up. This is great after a workout.

Vanilla Mocha Coffee

Ingredients: 5 heaping tbsps creamer/instant milk
1 pkg sweetener
1 heaping tbsp instant coffee
1 cup hot water

Directions: Very easy, very good. In an insert cup combine all the ingredients and mix well. Best with creamer or powdered milk from kitchen. You can drink it hot or cold. Either way, it is great.

Remember Bennigans

Ingredients: 2 tsps instant coffee   1 sweetener
                1 (.81 oz) Irish cream cappuccino
                1 tbsp chocolate syrup   1 cup hot water

Directions: This is the easiest recipe ever. In your coffee cup or insert cup, combine all these ingredients and stir well. Drink up!!

Yak Attack

Ingredients: ¼ (4 oz) bag instant coffee
                1 (12 oz) regular Mountain Dew
                1 (12 oz) Code Red soda
                1 (12 oz) Cherry Coke/Pepsi

Directions: Use a coffee cup and combine the instant coffee with about 10-12 tbsps of hot water. Mix this into a very thick syrup. Point of water is to melt the coffee. Pour the coffee syrup in either a container or a large spread bowl and pour in the sodas **slowly** one at a time. There will be a foam form as you add sodas. Stir slowly as you add sodas. Once all sodas are added grab your cup. Fill cup and slam drink. Do not sip but slam. Keep filling cup, keep slamming drink until all is gone. The hairs on your head will stand. What a rush!

O-G Cadillac

Ingredients: 1 heaping tbsp instant coffee
                3 heaping tbsps hot chocolate mix
                2 pkgs sweetener
                1 cup hot water

Directions: In a coffee cup or an insert cup, combine all ingredients. Mix well and drink up. Sit back and sip, just like the O-G's do it.

How About A Pretty

Ingredients: 12 pieces penny candies (different flavors)

4 butterscotch candies
1 heaping tbsp instant coffee
1 pkg sweetener
1 cup hot water

Directions: Crush all candies into small pieces and place in an insert cup. Now, add the coffee, sweetener, and hot water. Stir all well and place in a hot pot for 20 minutes so that all candies melt. Stir well and drink up. Great way to start off any day!

Hott Shot

Ingredients: 3 pieces fireball candies
1 heaping tbsp instant coffee
1 pkg sweetener
1 cup hot water

Directions: Break up the fireball candies and put in an insert cup. Add the coffee, sweetener, and hot water and stir well. Place cup in hot pot until candies melt, stir, and drink up. MMM Good! Both hot & spicy.

Mojo Tea

Ingredients: 8 fireball candies   7 tea bags
1 cup hot water   3 pkgs sweetener
3 (.14 oz) lemon lime sports drink/cooloffs
You will need: 3 (20 oz) empty water bottles

Directions: Crush all the fireballs and place in your insert cup. Add the seven tea bags with the cup of hot water. Place in a hot pot and heat for 45 minutes. Now remove the tea bags and equally divide the liquid between the three water bottles. Add one sweetener and one sports drink/cooloff to each bottle and shake well. Top off bottle with more hot water and shake again. Set the bottles aside and let cool down. Drink up and enjoy.

Classic Milkshake

Ingredients:　　8 butterscotch candies (optional)
　　　　　　　　1 pkg M&M's
　　　　　　　　1 pint vanilla ice cream　　½ (3.2 oz) pkg instant milk
　　　　　　　　1/3 cup cold water

Directions:　　Crush butterscotch candies into fairly small pieces and lightly crush up the M&M's. In a large spread bowl combine ice cream, instant milk, and cold water. Use two spoons and whip into a thick, yet creamy, mixture. Once whipped, add all candies and lightly whip again. That's it, drink up. Just like home.

Ice Cream Float

Ingredients:　　½ (3.2 oz) pkg instant milk　8 tbsps hot water
　　　　　　　　1 pint vanilla ice cream
　　　　　　　　1 (12 oz) Coca Cola

Directions:　　In a coffee cup combine the instant milk with the hot water and stir well. You want this thick and creamy. No lumps. Add a little water if needed. Now get a large cup and put half the ice cream in the cup with half the soda and half the instant milk. Stir just to mix lightly and drink. Do the same to the ice cream left in the container. Great on a hot day.

Caramel Root Beer Float

Ingredients:　　1 Milky Way candy bar　　1 pint vanilla ice cream
　　　　　　　　1 (12 oz) root beer soda

Directions:　　Cut Milky Way into small pieces and put in a hot pot insert. Place insert down in a hot pot to melt. Take half the ice cream from its container and put in a cup. Pour half the melted candy bar over the top of ice cream and slowly add the root beer soda until cup is full. Stir well and drink up. Pour the other half of the Milky Way over the ice cream in container, add root beer till container is full, and drink up. Quick, fast, and easy.

Strawberry Margaritas

Ingredients: 1 (12 oz) strawberry soda
                 8 (.14 oz) lemon lime sports drink/cooloffs
You will need: 6 (20 oz) empty water bottles

Directions: In a large spread bowl or a Gatorade bottle mix all
ingredients until the drink mix/cooloffs are dissolved. Equally divide
mixture between the water bottles and top off with cold water. Shake well.

Soups & Chowders

Sweet & Sour Soup

Ingredients:
2 cups hot water
4 pkgs sweeteners
12 tbsps pickle juice
2 (4 oz) servings carrots
1 heaping tsp black pepper
2 tbsps instant milk

Directions: In a clean chip bag combine all ingredients and place in a hot pot to heat for 4 hours. Great for a soar throat. Really, this is just a new idea as well as a new taste. If butter is available, grab some with your favorite crackers.

Spicy Vegetable Soup

Ingredients:
1 (4 oz) serving corn
1 (4 oz) serving green beans
1 (4 oz) serving carrots
1 tsp black pepper
1 pkg chili Ramen seasoning
2 cups hot water
½ tsp garlic powder
1 tbsp onion flakes

Directions: In a large clean chip bag, combine all the ingredients and place bag in a hot pot and heat for 6 full hours. Great on a cold day or a runny nose.

Cream of Tomato Soup

Ingredients:
1 (13.5 oz) bottle ketchup   1½ cups hot water
½ (3.2 oz) pkg instant milk   1 tbsp pepper
½ tsp salt

Directions: In a large clean chip bag, combine all ingredients and mix well. Place the bag in a hot pot and heat for 3 hours. Stir occasionally. You might need to add a little water as it cooks. Great dish on a cold day. Serve with saltine crackers and butter if available.

Tortilla Soup

Ingredients: 2 (3 oz) beef Ramen noodles   3 cups hot water
                1 (8 oz) pkg Mexican beef
                1 pkg beef Ramen seasoning
                ¼ (16 oz) bottle squeeze cheese   2 tbsps habanera sauce
                ½ (16 oz) bag tortilla chips

Directions: Cook noodles in a spread bowl using 3 cups of hot water. Wash off meat pack and place in a hot pot to heat. When hot, add to noodles along with beef seasoning pack and squeeze cheese. Mix well. Pour in habanera sauce and tortilla chips. Allow chips to soften and eat up.

Potato Soup

Ingredients: 1 (4 oz) pkg four cheese instant potato flakes
                1 (4 oz) pkg herb & butter instant potato flakes
                Hot water   1 (1.75 oz) bag pork skins
                1 (1.375 oz) pkg cheese & chive crackers
                ½ (3.2 oz) pkg instant milk   4 tbsps squeeze cheese
                2 (.75 oz) pkgs cream cheese

Directions: Use a spread bowl and combine all potato flakes with enough hot water to have a mixture that is thick like chowder. Stir until all lumps are gone. Crush pork skins and lightly crush crackers. Now combine all the rest of the ingredients and stir well. Pour this mixture into a clean chip bag and place in a hot pot. Thin with hot water to the consistency you desire. Leave in a hot pot to cook for 3 hours. Stir occasionally. This is a really great treat.

Another Potato Soup

Ingredients:
2 (1.3 oz) jalapeno peppers   1 (5 oz) summer sausage
2 (4 oz) pkgs instant potato flakes (any flavor)
1 tsp black pepper
3 (.75 oz) pkgs cream cheese
½ (3.2 oz) pkg instant milk
3 tbsps squeeze cheese   hot water
½ (8 oz) bag jalapeno chips

Directions: Cut up all jalapeno peppers and the summer sausage. Use a spread bowl and combine both packages potato flakes with enough water to have mixture that is thick like a chowder. Stir out all lumps. In a clean large chip bag combine potato flakes with the rest of the ingredients except for the jalapeno chips. Add enough hot water to get the consistency you desire. Place in a hot pot to heat for 2 hours. Open bag and add the jalapeno chips. Close bag and cook 15 minutes more. Check bag to make sure it is not too thick. If so, add water to thin. Cook for 1 ½ hours more. Once again, this is a great treat.

Chicken Noodle Soup

Ingredients:
2 tbsps starch (if available)
1 (7 oz) pkg chicken chunks
1 (1.3 oz) jalapeno pepper
1 pkg chicken Ramen seasoning
1 (4 oz) serving carrots
1 (3 oz) chicken Ramen noodles (not crushed)
2 cups hot water   3 tbsps squeeze cheese
4 tbsps instant milk

Directions: If starch is available, whip until all chunks are gone. In a clean chip bag combine all ingredients, mix well, and place in a hot pot. Heat for 3 to 4 hours. Great on a cold day or when you may be a little under the weather. Grab your saltines and favorite drink.

Baltimore's Beef Stew

Ingredients: 3 tbsps starch (if available)   2 pkgs beef Ramen seasoning
1 (4 oz) serving green beans   1 (8 oz) pkg beef tips
1 (4 oz) serving carrots
1 (8 oz) serving ground beef from tray
2 cups hot water   1 heaping tbsp onion flakes
1 (4 oz) serving corn   2 tbsps instant milk

Directions: If you have the starch, mix until all lumps are gone. Get a clean chip bag and combine all ingredients, stir well, and place in a hot pot to heat for 3 to 4 hours. Once ready, fill your bowl and enjoy. This is great with some buttered rice or instant potatoes.

Mackerel Chowder

Ingredients: 1 (1.3 oz) jalapeno pepper   1 (3.5 oz) pkg mackerel
3 tbsps instant milk   2 (.75 oz) pkgs cream cheese
1 (3 oz) chicken Ramen noodles & seasoning pkg
1 cup hot water

Directions: Cut up the jalapeno pepper and put in a large clean chip bag. Add all the rest of the ingredients to bag with 1 cup hot water. Place bag in a hot pot to heat for 1½ hours. If mixture gets too dry, add water to keep chowder consistency. If you add more water, add a little instant milk as well. Really nice change.

Fish Stew

Ingredients: 3 (3.5 oz) pkgs mackerel   1 (12 oz) V-8 juice
1 (11.25 oz) pkg beef stew   2 tbsps hot sauce
2 pkgs chili Ramen seasoning
1 pkg beef Ramen seasoning
2 (1.3 oz) jalapeno peppers   ½ (9 oz) pickle
1 (5 oz) summer sausage   1 (3 oz) beef Ramen noodles
½ (8 oz) bag rice   2 flour tortillas
1 tsp squeeze cheese

Directions: In a coffee cup drain all juice from mackerel. Set mackerels aside. In a clean large chip bag combine mackerel juice, V-8 juice, beef stew package, hot sauce, and all three seasoning packages. Now cut up the jalapeno peppers, pickle, and half the summer sausage. Add them to mixture in bag and mix well. Place this bag in a hot pot to heat for 1 hour. In a large spread bowl combine beef Ramen noodles, rice, and mackerels. Cut up other half of the summer sausage and tear flour tortillas into pieces. Add them to spread bowl. Add hot water to bowl until it is 1 inch above mixture and cover bowl. Remove bag from hot pot, pour into bowl, and mix well. Top off with squeeze cheese and stir. Invite your homeboy. Feeds two.

Pork Stew

Ingredients: 1 (3 oz) pkg spam   1 (1.75 oz) bag pork skins
¼ (3 oz) bottle onion flakes   ½ tsp garlic powder
1 (4 oz) serving corn   1 pkg shrimp Ramen seasoning
1 (4 oz) serving green beans   2 cups hot water

Directions: Cut up spam into fairly small pieces. Crush pork skins lightly. Grab a chip bag and combine all ingredients and mix well. Place this bag in a hot pot and cook for 6 hours. You can add just a shot of squeeze cheese, but you really do not need it. Great with a side of potatoes.

Dips & Cream Spreads

Salsa

Ingredients:
- 2 (9 oz) pickles (reg or hot)
- 10 (1.3 oz) jalapeno peppers
- 1 (3 oz) bottle onion flakes   1 tsp garlic powder
- 1 (12 oz) V-8 juice   1 (5 oz) bottle habanera sauce

Directions: Cut up pickles and jalapeno peppers. In a large chip bag combine all the ingredients and mix well. Place this bag in a hot pot to heat for 6 hours. Pour the mixture into a clean peanut butter jar. Let sit 48 hours before you eat. Can also add chili Ramen seasoning package for a spicier salsa. Great on meals, chips, and crackers.

Tartar Sauce

Ingredients:
- 1 (14 oz) jar salad dressing   4 tbsps pickle juice
- ½ (8 oz) jar relish   ½ tsp onion powder

Directions: In a spread bowl combine all ingredients and mix well. Will use two jars now. Spoon the mixture back into jars and use on your favorite meals.

Guacamole

Ingredients:
- 1 (6 oz) bag salsa Verde chips
- 1 (1.375 oz) pkg cheese & chive crackers
- 1 (1.3 oz) jalapeno pepper   2 (.75 oz) pkgs cream cheese

3 tbsps pickle juice   6 tbsps squeeze cheese

Directions: Crush up the chips and crackers into a fine powder. Combine all the ingredients and mix very well. If too dry for your taste, add a little more pickle juice and cream cheese. Enjoy this one with your favorite chips.

My French Onion Dip

Ingredients: 3 (.75 oz) pkgs cream cheese
                  1 pkg chili Ramen seasoning
                  3 tbsps pickle juice   1 pkg beef Ramen seasoning
                  1 pkg chicken Ramen seasoning

Directions: You will only use ½ the chili Ramen seasoning package and ½ the chicken Ramen seasoning package. Combine all the ingredients and mix well. To make taste stronger, add a little more of the left-over seasoning.

Cheesy & Spicy Bean Dip

Ingredients: 1 (12 oz) bag refried beans   2 (1.3 oz) jalapeno peppers
                  ¼ (16 oz) bottle squeeze cheese   2 tbsps habanera sauce

Directions: Using a spread bowl, cook the refried beans but leave on the thick side. As beans cook, cut the jalapeno peppers into fine pieces. When beans are done, combine the rest of the ingredients and mix well. Once all is mixed, grab your chips and a friend or two.

Cream Cheese Spread

Ingredients: 1 (16 oz) pkg Duplex cookies
                  15 (.75 oz) pkgs cream cheese
                  1/3 cup instant milk
                  1/3 cup hot chocolate mix   1/3 cup hot water
                  ½ (8 oz) pkg Regal graham cookies

Directions: Separate cream from cookies and set cookies aside. In a spread bowl, combine cream from cookies, cream cheese, instant milk, hot chocolate mix, and the hot water. Mix well. Crush Regal graham cookies and sprinkle over the top of the spread. Spoon cream cheese spread on Duplex cookies and eat. Pretty good treat with hot coffee.

Chocolate-Peanut Butter Cream Spread

Ingredients: 3 tbsps hot chocolate mix   1 tbsp peanut butter
                 3 (.75 oz) pkgs cream cheese   2 tbsps hot water
                 1 (5.6 oz) pkg Maria cookies

Directions: In a spread bowl combine hot chocolate mix, peanut butter, cream cheese, and hot water. Mix thoroughly until smooth and creamy. Spread the mixture over the cookies and eat. Really nice snack. If Maria cookies are not available, you can substitute with vanilla wafers.

Soy Sauce

Ingredients: 1 pkg beef Ramen seasoning   ¼ cup hot water
                 ¼ tsp coffee

Directions: Combine all ingredients in a coffee cup and mix well. Make sure all are dissolved. Might need to adjust a little to suit taste. Great on meals and rice dishes.

Side Dishes

Hot Jalapeno Bombers

Ingredients:
10 (1.3 oz) jalapeno peppers   ¼ (8 oz) bag rice
1 (8 oz) pkg Mexican beef   2 pkgs chili Ramen seasoning
4 (.75 oz) pkgs cream cheese   ¼ cup salsa
2 handfuls jalapeno chips   2 handfuls corn chips

Directions: Cut stem out of jalapeno peppers and clean out seeds. Set peppers aside. In a spread bowl, cook rice about halfway, then drain any remaining water. Stir in the Mexican beef, chili Ramen seasoning, 3 packages of the cream cheese, and salsa. Mix well. Crush the jalapeno chips very finely and add to the mixture. Mix well again. Carefully fill the jalapeno peppers with the mixture. Once all are filled, crush the corn chips into a fine powder. With remaining cream cheese pack, coat the jalapeno peppers and roll into crushed corn chips. Wrap each pepper into a clean white sheet of paper. Once all are wrapped, place them in a clean chip bag, place into hot pot, and cook for 2 full hours. These are both juicy as well as delicious.

Stuffed Pickles

Ingredients: 4 (9 oz) pickles   1 (4.23 oz) pkg tuna
1 pkg Ramen chili seasoning   3 tbsps pickle juice
¼ tbsp mustard   1 pkg sweetener
½ (14 oz) jar salad dressing   hot sauce to taste
¼ (6 oz) bag salsa Verde chips

¼ (1.75 oz) bag pork skins   ¼ (8 oz) bag jalapeno chips
1 (1.25 oz) bag hot fries

Directions: Cut pickles in half lengthwise and clean out all seeds. Set jalapeno chips and hot fries aside. Combine all the rest of the ingredients in your spread bowl and mix well. Let this mixture sit for 30 minutes. Now crush chips and hot fries, add to mixture and stir. Use this mixture to fill pickle halves. If you have any cheese puffs, crush a handful and top off pickles. If there is any leftover mixture, break out some nacho or tortilla chips. Wash down all with your favorite drink.

Stuffed Jalapenos

Ingredients: 20 (1.3 oz) jalapeno peppers
1 (11.25 oz) pkg chili no beans
1 (8 oz) pkg Mexican ground beef
1 cup refried beans   1 cup jalapeno chips
8 (.75 oz) pkgs cream cheese
¼ (16 oz) bottle squeeze cheese   1 cup party mix

Directions: Cut the jalapeno peppers in half lengthwise and clean out the seeds. Rinse both meat packs and place in a hot pot to heat. While heating meat packs, prepare refried beans and crush the jalapeno chips. Once meat packs are hot, in a spread bowl, combine refried beans, meat packs, jalapeno chips, cream cheese, and squeeze cheese. Mix very well. Now, carefully fill jalapeno halves with mixture. Once all halves have been filled, crush party mix and top. If you have any mixture left, break out some nacho or tortilla chips and enjoy. Trust that every bite is simply delicious.

Tahitian Rice

Ingredients: 1/3 onion (sub 2 tbsps onion flakes)
2 tbsps homemade soy sauce
¼ cup melted butter   1½ tbsps mustard
¼ cup brown sugar   1½ tbsps cornstarch
¾ pkg chicken Ramen seasoning
1 (4 oz) serving fruit cocktail/pineapple

1 cup rice	1 (12 oz) any type fruit juice
1 tsp black pepper	1 (2 oz) pkg energy mix

Directions: As you can see, you will need a little help from the kitchen for this recipe. Cut up the onion and mix up the homemade soy sauce (recipe in the book) Set the energy mix aside till the end. Use a clean chip bag and combine all these ingredients with ¼ cup of hot water. Place the bag in a hot pot to cook for 3½ hours. Stir it occasionally. If mixture gets too dry, add a little water. When done, pour off any remaining juices, pour mixture into a spread bowl, and top with energy mix. Stir well. This is a great dish to eat with mackerel or any fish dish. Any way you eat it, you'll love it. Other Tahitian dishes call for dish to marinade, this dish does not need to marinade. Enjoy!

Home-Style Hash Browns

Ingredients: 5 (1.25 oz) small bags hot fries   1 (3 oz) pkg spam
1½ tbsps pickle juice   2 tbsps refried beans
¼ (3 oz) chili Ramen noodles
¼ pkg chili Ramen seasoning   ketchup to taste
hot sauce to taste   squeeze cheese to taste

Directions: Crush hot fries lightly and finely dice spam. In your spread bowl combine hot fries, spam, pickle juice, refried beans, chili Ramen noodles, and the seasoning package. Stir in 1/3 cup of hot water and mix well. Put mixture in a clean chip bag and place in a hot pot. Cook for 1 to 1 ½ hours. When finished, put hash browns in your spread bowl and top off with ketchup, hot sauce, and cheese. Just like home, right?

Deviled Eggs

Ingredients: 6 hardboiled eggs   1 tbsp salad dressing
1 tsp mustard   1 tbsp relish
1 pinch pepper   1 pkg chili Ramen seasoning

Directions: Peel and rinse eggs, cut in half. Remove yokes and put in a small bowl. Smash yokes and add salad dressing, mustard, relish, and pepper. Mix well. Spoon mixture back into egg halves and sprinkle with chili Ramen seasoning. Just like home!

Egg Salad

Ingredients:
6 hardboiled eggs	1 tbsp onion flakes
¾ tbsp pickle juice	1 ½ tbsps salad dressing
1 tsp pepper	1 tbsp relish
1 tsp mustard	¼ tsp salt
½ tsp garlic powder	

Directions: Cut up all hardboiled eggs and put in a spread bowl. Use a little hot water to hydrate the onion flakes. Now add all ingredients to the spread bowl and mix well. Serve on bread, crackers, or tortilla chips.

Not Just Potatoes

Ingredients:
- 1 (5 oz) summer sausage
- 1 (4 oz) pkg instant potato flakes (any flavor)
- 2 (.75 oz) pkgs cream cheese   1tbsp onion flakes
- ½ tsp garlic powder
- 3 (1.375 oz) pkgs cheese & chive crackers

Directions: Cut summer sausage into tiny pieces. In a spread bowl cook potato flakes in just enough hot water to hydrate. Stir in summer sausage, cream cheese, onion flakes, and garlic powder. Mix well and put mixture in a chip bag. Place this bag in a hot pot to cook for 2 hours. Remove from hot pot and pour into a spread bowl. Crush up crackers and top. MMM MMM Good!

Side of Potatoes

Ingredients:
- 1 (5 oz) summer sausage (diced)
- 2 (1.375 oz) pkgs cheese & chive crackers
- 1 (4 oz) pkg four cheese instant potato flakes
- 2 tbsps squeeze cheese

1 (1.3 oz) jalapeno pepper (diced)

Directions: Cut your summer sausage into fairly small pieces and crush up crackers. Follow instructions on package to cook the cheese potato flakes. Once potatoes are cooked add two tbsps of hot water then add the rest of your ingredients. Add a spoon of butter if available. Mix all well and eat up.

Perfect Pickling

Ingredients: 1 (9 oz) dill pickle   1 (1.3 oz) jalapeno pepper
                 2 (.34 oz) lemon lime sports drink/cooloff

Directions: Cut the pickle and jalapeno pepper into fairly small pieces. Get an empty peanut butter jar. Pour the pickle juice into the peanut butter jar, add the sport drink/cooloff, and stir until all is dissolved. Put all the pickle and jalapeno pieces in the jar and let sit for 3 days. Take out and shake from time to time.

Beef, Cheese, & Potatoes

Ingredients: 1 (1.3 oz) jalapeno pepper
                 1 serving pkg beef & cheese sticks
                 1 (4 oz) pkg four cheese instant potato flakes
                 ¼ pkg beef Ramen seasoning

Directions: Cut up the jalapeno pepper and the beef and cheese stick. In a spread bowl cook the potato flakes according to directions. Once cooked, add the rest of the ingredients and mix well. Nothing left to do now but eat. Great side dish with your favorite meal.

Columbian Rice

Ingredients: ¼ (8 oz) bag rice   1 (3 oz) chili Ramen noodles
                 1 tbsp salad dressing   1 (1.5 oz) pkg ranch dressing
                 1 tbsp soy sauce   2 (1.3 oz) jalapeno peppers
                 1 (sleeve) pkg saltine crackers

Directions: In a clean large chip bag combine rice, noodles, salad
dressing, ranch dressing, and soy sauce. If no soy sauce is available, see
recipe for it in this book. Add enough water to bag to allow rice and noodles
to cook. Cut up jalapeno peppers, add to mixture, and stir well. Place bag in
a hot pot and cook for 1 hour. After cook time, stir in seasoning package that
came with the noodles. Pour all into a spread bowl. Unless you are really
hungry, you can invite a friend to join you.

Spanish Rice

Ingredients: 1 (12 oz) V-8 juice   1 (8 oz) pkg Mexican beef
                 ¼ (8 oz) bag rice   1 (4 oz) serving corn from tray
                 ¼ tsp onion powder   4 tbsps salsa

Directions: Combine all ingredients, except salsa, in a chip bag and
place in a hot pot to cook for 45 minutes. When done, pour all into spread
bowl and stir in the salsa. Nice little side dish

Sweet & Sour Rice

Ingredients: ½ (8 oz) bag rice
                 1 (12 oz) pineapple orange juice
                 3 tbsps pickle juice
                 2 pkgs sweetener

Directions: In a clean chip bag combine rice and pineapple juice, place
in a hot pot and cook for 45 minutes. Remove from hot pot and pour out any
excess juice. Place rice in a spread bowl and quickly add the pickle juice and
sweeteners. Stir well and eat while good and hot. If you desire, you can also
add some mixed fruit to mixture after cooked.

Down & Out Dirty Rice

Ingredients: 1 (3.5 oz) pkg mackerel   1 (5 oz) summer sausage
                 1 (11.25 oz) pkg chili no beans   ¾ (8 oz) bag rice
                 2 (1.3 oz) jalapeno peppers   ¼ (9 oz) pickle
                 1 cup jalapeno chips   ½ pkg chili Ramen seasoning
                 1 (2 oz) pkg hot peanuts
You will need: 2 hot pots

Directions: Drain juices from mackerel and cut up summer sausage. In a clean chip bag, combine chili, mackerel, and the cut up summer sausage. Place this in a hot pot to heat for 30 minutes. Right before this is done, grab a spread bowl and cook the rice. Drain any water. Now cut up the jalapeno pepper, pickle, and crush the jalapeno chips. When rice is done and all is cut up, combine all the ingredients in the chip bag except the jalapeno chips. Put bag back in the hot pot and cook for 1 ½ hours. Remove the bag from the hot pot and stir in the chips. Cover and let sit for 10 minutes. Now it is time to get down and dirty. Enjoy. If your unit only sells summer sausage at the Christmas season, you can use beef tips.

Sweet & Sour Summer Sausage

Ingredients: 6 tbsps pickle juice   2 pkgs beef Ramen seasoning
                 ½ tbsp coffee   1 (5 oz) summer sausage
                 2 (4 oz) lemon pies   ½ (8 oz) bag of rice
                 1 (.14 oz) pkg orange sports drink/cooloff
                 2 (1.75 oz) bags pork skins

Directions: Use an insert cup and combine pickle juice, beef Ramen seasoning packages, and coffee. Stir and place in a hot pot to heat for 30 minutes. Cut the summer sausage into small pieces and put in a small, clean chip bag. Remove the lemon filling from the pies and add to the summer sausage. Place this in a hot pot with insert cup. While both of them heat, pour rice into a bowl and stir in 1 cup of hot water and cook half way, about

3 minutes. Now, stir in the orange sports drink/cooloff and recover. When rice is done, divide into two bowls. Remove insert cup and bag from hot pot and divide both equally between the two bowls. In each bowl stir in the pork skins. Cover 5 minutes and eat up.

Mackerel Salad

Ingredients:
1 (3.5 oz) pkg mackerel   2 hard boiled eggs
1 (1.3 oz) jalapeno pepper   1 tbsp relish
1 tsp black pepper   1 tbsp onion flakes
2 tbsps squeeze cheese   2 tbsps salad dressing

Directions: Drain the package of mackerel. Cut hard boiled eggs into small pieces and set aside. Also cut up the jalapeno pepper. Now, in a spread bowl, combine all ingredients, except the eggs, and mix well. Once all is mixed, add the eggs and lightly stir again. This is best served on saltine crackers. Now grab yourself a cold drink. Enjoy!

Tuna Salad

Ingredients:
1 heaping tbsp onion flakes   3 hard boiled eggs
¼ (9 oz) dill pickle   1 (4.23 oz) pkg tuna
1 tsp black pepper   1 heaping tbsp relish
2 tbsps salad dressing
½ pkg chicken/chili Ramen seasoning
1 tsp garlic powder   4 tbsps pickle juice

Directions: Using hot water hydrate the onion flakes. Dice up the hard boiled eggs and set aside. Dice pickle into small pieces. Grab a spread bowl and mix all the ingredients thoroughly except the eggs. Add eggs and lightly mix again. Eat this on bread, chips, or crackers. Grab your favorite drink and eat up.

Tahitian Tuna

Ingredients: 1/3 onion (sub 2 tbsps onion flakes)
2 tbsps soy sauce   ¼ cup melted butter
1½ tbsps mustard   1 tbsp garlic powder
1 (4.23 oz) pkg tuna   1 tbsp coriander & annatto
1 (12 oz) strawberry kiwi/fruit juice
1 (4 oz) serving fruit cocktail from tray
1 (2 oz) pkg energy mix

Directions: Cut up onion if available and prepare soy sauce (see recipe in the book). Set the energy mix to the side. Use a clean chip bag and combine all the ingredients. Tie up bag and marinade for 3 hours. Once marinated, place bag in a hot pot and cook for another 3 hours. Once done, drain all juices from tuna mixture, put all in a spread bowl, add the energy mix, stir well, and enjoy each and every bite. Left over juices can be poured over rice. If you eat rice with this dish, save a little energy mix for it.

Jack Mack Fiesta

Ingredients: 1 (3 oz) chicken Ramen noodles   ½ (8 oz) bag rice
½ (9 oz) pickle (reg/hot)   2 (1.3 oz) jalapeno peppers
½ (1.75 oz) bag pork skins   1 (5 oz) summer sausage
3 (3.5 oz) pkgs mackerel
2 pkgs chicken Ramen seasoning
1 (1.5 oz) pkg ranch dressing   1 (2 oz) pkg hot peanuts
¼ (16 oz) bottle squeeze cheese

Directions: This will be a cold dish. In a spread bowl cook noodles and rice without any seasoning. After they cook, drain and rinse well. Set aside to cool. Cut up the pickle and jalapeno peppers. Crush pork skins and dice the summer sausage. Drain the mackerel and combine all the ingredients in a spread bowl and mix well. To take away some of the fish taste, add a shot of pickle juice and a little pepper. MMM Good!!

Tahitian Mackerel

Ingredients:
2 tbsps soy sauce
1 (3.5 oz) pkg mackerel   1½ tbsps mustard
1 (12 oz) orange juice   1½ tbsps corn starch
1 (.34 oz) pkg lemon lime sports drink
1 (4 oz) serving fruit cocktail/pineapple
1/3 onion (sub 2 tbsps onion flakes)
¼ cup melted butter   ¼ cup brown sugar
1 (2 oz) pkg energy mix

Directions: As you can see from the ingredients, you will need a little help from the kitchen. For soy sauce use recipe in the book. Now set aside the energy mix. Use a clean chip bag and combine all ingredients. Tie off bag and marinade for 3 hours. After it is marinated, place bag in a hot pot and cook for an additional 3 hours. Once done, drain juices in a coffee cup. Pour the mixture in a spread bowl. Add energy mix to bowl and stir well. This meal is great with a side order of rice. Use the leftover juices in cup to pour over rice. If you eat rice with this dish, save a few pieces from energy mix to top off. Amazing meal.

Sweet & Sour Mackerel & Rice

Ingredients:
1 (1.3 oz) jalapeno pepper   1 (3.5 oz) pkg mackerel
2 pkgs sweetener   ½ (8 oz) bag rice
2 tsps pickle juice
1 (12 oz) pineapple orange juice

Directions: Cut jalapeno pepper into small pieces. Drain mackerel. In a large clean chip bag, combine all ingredients and stir well. Place this bag in a hot pot to heat for 30 minutes, stirring occasionally. Take bag out and stir well. If dry, add a tbsp or two of hot water. Place back in the hot pot for another 30 minutes. Simply delicious!

Tuna Wraps

Ingredients: ¼ (9 oz) pickle
2 (1.3 oz) jalapeno peppers 3 tbsps refried beans
2 tbsps onion flakes   ½ pkg shrimp Ramen seasoning
1 (4.23 oz) pkg tuna   1 (27.2 oz) pkg flour tortillas
¼ (16 oz) bottle squeeze cheese
3 (.75 oz) pkgs cream cheese   ¼ (12 oz) bottle salsa
1 (1.5 oz) pkg ranch dressing   ½ (8 oz) bag BBQ chips

Directions: Cut up pickle and jalapeno peppers and set aside. In a spread bowl, combine refried beans, onion flakes, Ramen seasoning, and pickle. Drain tuna and add to bowl. Mix well. Separate flour tortillas and cover all with squeeze cheese. In a coffee cup mix all 3 packages of cream cheese with 2 tbsps salsa and stir well. Combine this mixture with the tuna mixture and mix well. Spoon this mixture onto the flour tortillas and roll into your wraps. Place 4 wraps in a small chip bag and place in a hot pot for 2½ hours. When cook time is up, place 4 wraps into a spread bowl and cover all with ranch dressing, salsa, and jalapeno peppers. Eat with the BBQ chips and favorite drink. This is a great meal to share with a close friend.

Zee Mack Patty #1

Ingredients: 1 (3.5 oz) pkg mackerel
4 cheese & chive crackers from 1 (1.375 oz) pkg
2 (1.3 oz) jalapeno peppers
1 (1.5 oz) pkg ranch dressing
½ (9 oz) pickle   4 pieces bread
Squeeze cheese to taste   Salad dressing to taste

Directions: Drain most of the juice from the mackerel package. Crush crackers and cut up jalapeno peppers. In a spread bowl combine the mackerel, ranch dressing, and crackers. Mix well. Stir in the jalapeno pepper pieces and divide mixture into two equal parts. Form your patties out of these. Get two small chip bags and place one patty in each bag. Now place the bags in a hot pot to cook for 1 ½ hours. While waiting, cut up the pickle. When cook time is up, remove from hot pot and bags; put patties on bread and top with pickles, salad dressing, and squeeze cheese. Zee that? Good huh? Wash all down with favorite drink.

Zee Mack Patty #2

Ingredients: 1 (3.5 oz) pkg mackerel
2 (1.3 oz) jalapeno peppers
4 sour cream & onion crackers from 1 (1.375) pkg
1 (.75 oz) pkg cream cheese
4 pieces bread
ketchup to taste

Directions: Drain most of the juice from the mackerel package. Cut up the jalapeno peppers and crush the crackers. In a spread bowl combine the mackerel, cream cheese, crackers, and diced jalapeno peppers. Mix well and divide mixture into two equal parts. Form your patties out of these. Get two small chip bags and place one patty in each bag. Now place the bags in a hot pot to cook for 1 ½ hours. After cook time, remove bags from hot pot and patties from bags. Put the patties on bread and top with ketchup. You can use a shot of squeeze cheese if you desire. Break out your chips and favorite drink. It's time to eat!

Zee Mack Patty #3

Ingredients: 2 (1.3 oz) jalapeno peppers   ½ (1.75 oz) bag pork skins
1 (3.5 oz) pkg mackerel   1 pkg chili Ramen seasoning
1 tbsp hot water
1 (1.375 oz) pkg cheese & chive crackers
4 pieces bread   Salad dressing to taste

Directions: Do not drain this mackerel. Cut up the jalapeno peppers and crush pork skins. In a spread bowl combine mackerel, pork skins. seasoning, and jalapeno peppers. Mix well. Now crush up the crackers and knead into mixture. If too dry, add a tbsp of hot water. Once mixed well, separate mixture into 2 equal parts and form your patties. Place one patty in a small chip bag and do the same with the other. Place the bags in a hot pot to heat for 1 ½ hours. When finished, remove patties from the bags and place on bread. Top off with salad dressing. Once again break out your favorite chips and drink. Enjoy!

Cellblock Cuisine

Ingredients: 2 (3 oz) chili Ramen noodles
1 (3.5 oz) mackerel or (4.23 oz) tuna
1 (9 oz) pickle
1 (4 oz) serving mixed fruit
1 (.34 oz) lemon lime sports drink/cooloff
¼ cup sunflower seeds

Directions: Cook the noodles and rinse well with cold water. Drain the mackerel/tuna, cut up pickle, and dice the fruit. Place the noodles, mackerel, and pickle in a chip bag and place in a hot pot for 45 minutes. After cook time, pour mixture into a spread bowl and add cooloff/sports drink mix, fruit, and sunflower seeds. Mix well and eat while hot.

Fish Creole

Ingredients: 1 (4.23 oz) pkg tuna   1 (3.5 oz) pkg mackerel
¼ pkg chili Ramen seasoning
¼ pkg shrimp Ramen seasoning
1 (4 oz) heaping serving okra
1 (4 oz) serving green beans
1 tsp onion powder   2 tbsps salsa
1/3 cup water

Directions: Drain juices from tuna and mackerel. In a large chip bag combine all the ingredients with 1/3 cup of water and place in a hot pot to cook for 2 hours. Pour into a spread bowl and eat with saltines or tortilla chips.

Fish Sticks

Ingredients: 1 (3.5 oz) pkg mackerel   1 (4.23 oz) pkg tuna

¼ (1.5 oz) pkg ranch dressing   1 cup jalapeno chips
¼ (16 oz) bag corn chips

Directions: Drain the mackerel and tuna packages. In a spread bowl combine mackerel, tuna, and ranch dressing. Mix well. Crush jalapeno chips, add to mixture, and knead. Set aside. Crush the corn chips and add enough hot water, so you can knead and they stick together. Flatten in the chip bag and cut open. Cut this mixture with your ID card into 6" x 8" squares. Spoon fish mixture onto squares and roll up. Place these sticks in a small chip bag and place in a hot pot to cook for 3 hours. Put all in a spread bowl and top with tartar sauce. See recipe in Dip & Cream Spreads. You gotta love em'.

Super-Seas Delight

Ingredients: ½ (9 oz) pickle   3 (1.3 oz) jalapeno peppers
                 1 (3.5 oz) pkg mackerel   1 (3.53 oz) pkg sardines
                 1 (4.23 oz) pkg tuna   ½ cup salsa
                 ½ cup squeeze cheese   2 tbsps hot sauce
                 2 (2 oz) pkgs trail mix   2 tbsps pickle juice
                 3 tbsps salad dressing   1 (27.2 oz) pkg flour tortillas
You will need: 2 hot pots

Directions: Cut up pickle and jalapeno peppers and put in a spread bowl. Drain juices from all meat packages. Pour meat packages into a spread bowl and add the rest of the ingredients except the flour tortillas. Mix well. Spoon the mixture onto the tortillas and roll up. Place 4 tortillas in a chip bag and place in a hot pot to heat for 45 minutes. Use a couple hot pots for all to be done at the same time. Make some refried beans as a side dish or eat with favorite chips and a cold drink.

BBQ Mackerel

Ingredients: ¼ (8 oz) bag rice   2 (3.5 oz) pkgs mackerel
                 ½ (9 oz) dill pickle   1 cup jalapeno chips
                 2 tbsps onion flakes   1 heaping tbsp salad dressing
                 ½ (18 oz) bottle BBQ sauce   1 tsp mustard

¼ (16 oz) bottle squeeze cheese   2 tbsps pickle juice
5 tbsps refried beans   1 (27.2 oz) pkg flour tortillas

Directions: Pour rice in a spread bowl and cook. While rice is cooking drain mackerel packages, cut up pickle, and crush chips. When spread bowl with rice is ready, combine all ingredients, except flour tortillas, and mix well. Refried beans will cook inside wraps. Separate the flour tortillas and spoon mixture onto these. Roll all up and place 4 in a chip bag and place in a hot pot for 1 hour. Remove from hot pot and eat. Can coat with more cheese if you wish. You will not believe how great this tastes.

Quick Snack

Ingredients: 1 (11.25 oz) pkg chili no beans
1 (11.25 oz) pkg shredded beef in BBQ sauce
1 (12 oz) bag refried beans   2 (1.3 oz) jalapeno peppers
¼ (16 oz) bottle squeeze cheese
1 (16 oz) bag tortilla chips

Directions: Rinse meat packages and place in a hot pot to heat. In a spread bowl cook the refried beans. Cut up the jalapeno peppers and add peppers and cheese to bean mixture and stir well. When meat packs are hot, pour into bean mixture and stir again. You can eat this recipe two ways. Eat as a dip with chips, or layer bowl with chips and mixture. Repeat until mixture is gone. Quick, fast, and good.

Smothered Potatoes

Ingredients: 1 (1.3 oz) jalapeno pepper
1 (11.25 oz) pkg shredded beef in BBQ sauce
½ tsp onion powder
1 (4 oz) pkg instant potato flakes (any flavor)

Directions: Cut up jalapeno pepper, rinse off meat package, add pepper pieces to package and add onion powder. Mix this up and place in a hot pot to heat for 1 hour. When meat package is good and hot, pour instant potatoes into a spread bowl and use enough hot water just to hydrate potatoes. Pile

potatoes in the center of the spread bowl and pour meat package over top.
Sounds really simple, and it is really good.

Cheese Steak Sandwich

Ingredients: 1 (11.25 oz) pkg shredded beef in BBQ sauce
2 tbsps onion flakes   ½ (9 oz) pickle
1 (1.3 oz) jalapeno pepper   4 pieces bread
2 tbsps salad dressing   2 tbsps squeeze cheese
salt and pepper to taste

Directions: Separate beef pieces from BBQ sauce and rinse beef pieces.
Set the BBQ sauce aside. In a clean chip bag combine the beef pieces, 3
tbsps water, and onion flakes. Place the bag in a hot pot to heat for 1 hour.
When ready, pour off any water. Now, cut up the pickle and jalapeno
pepper. Split beef into two equal parts. Put half on one piece of bread and
the other half on another piece of bread. Top off with pickle, jalapeno
pepper, cheese, salad dressing, and salt and pepper. Break out the party mix
and favorite drink. If you do not want to waste BBQ sauce, mix up some
instant potatoes and top with BBQ sauce.

Sweet & Sour Summer Sausage

Ingredients: 2 pkgs beef Ramen seasoning   ½ tbsp instant coffee
½ cup pickle juice
1 (.34 oz) orange sports drink mix/cooloff
½ (8 oz) bag rice   2 (4 oz) lemon pies
1 (5 oz) summer sausage   2 (1.75 oz) small bags pork skins

Directions: In a clean chip bag combine both Ramen seasoning
packages, coffee, and pickle juice. Stir well and place bag in a hot pot to
heat for 30 minutes. In a coffee or insert cup mix sports drink/cooloff with ¾
cup hot water and pour into rice. Cover rice and cook fully. While waiting,
remove lemon filling from pies and cut up summer sausage into small
pieces. Place both in a small chip bag and place in hot pot with other bag.
Heat for 1 hour. When all is ready, split rice into two spread bowls and split
contents of both bags between bowls and mix well. Crush pork skins lightly

and add one bag to each bowl. Stir, cover, and let sit for 10 minutes. You won't believe the taste.

Big Baller Burgers

Ingredients: 2 (11.25 oz) pkgs shredded beef in BBQ sauce
5 (1.3 oz) jalapeno peppers   1 (8 oz) bag jalapeno chips
2 (9 oz) pickles   1 loaf of bread
Cheese to taste   hot sauce to taste
Salad dressing to taste

Directions: Rinse the meat packs, open, and place in a hot pot. Dice the jalapeno peppers and add to meat packs. Heat for 1 hour. While waiting, crush jalapeno chips and dice the pickles. Set aside. After cook time, pour meat packs into crushed chips and knead. Flatten in bag like a pizza. Wrap in paper and let sit for 15 minutes. Unwrap, cut open bag, and cut mixture into squares to fit on bread. Put squares on bread and top with pickles, cheese, hot sauce, and salad dressing. If onion is available, add to the toppings. Only big ballers need to eat this one :) !!!

Baltimore's Beef Pot Pie

Ingredients: 1 (16 oz) bag vanilla wafers   8 flour tortillas
1 (4 oz) serving green beans
1 pkg beef Ramen seasoning
2 (8 oz) servings ground beef from tray
3 tbsps squeeze cheese
1 (4 oz) serving carrots   1 tsp onion powder
1 tsp onion flakes   ½ tsp garlic powder
1 (11.25 oz) pkg shredded beef in BBQ sauce or sub (8 oz) beef tips

Directions: Crush all vanilla wafers as fine as possible and place 2/3 of the bag in a spread bowl. Spoon in enough water (3 ½ to 4 tbsps) to knead into a moist dough. Flatten dough in the bottom of a spread bowl and work dough into a pie crust. Now, take 4 of the tortillas and cover the vanilla wafers. Set bowl aside. Put the rest of the wafers in a separate bowl and add

1 ½ to 2 tbsps of water and knead into a dough. Flatten in the bottom of a spread bowl and set aside. This will go over pie as a top. In a clean chip bag, combine the rest of the ingredients except the flour tortillas. Place the bag in a hot pot to cook for 2 hours. Best to double bag unless you use a rice bag. Once done, stir and pour into the pie crust and cover with the last 4 flour tortillas. Put final piece of dough on top and pinch all around to create the pot pie. Grab your spoon and dig in. You have one delicious meal here.

Chip and Cheese Burger

Ingredients: 1 (6 oz) small bag salsa Verde chips
1 (8 oz) pkg Mexican beef   2 tbsps refried beans
¼ (9 oz) pickle   1 (1.3 oz) jalapeno pepper
1 tsp onion flakes   4 slices bread
2 tbsps squeeze cheese   1 heaping tbsp salad dressing
hot sauce to taste

Directions: Crush salsa Verde chips. Add Mexican beef and refried beans to bag with 2 to 3 tbsps of water and knead together well. Separate mixture into 2 equal parts. Pat mixture into patties and place 1 in a small chip bag and the other in another bag. Place both bags in a hot pot and heat for 2 hours. Cut pickle and jalapeno pepper into pieces and hydrate onion flakes in a little water. When burgers are done, coat bread with squeeze cheese. Dress up with pickle and jalapeno pieces. Top all off with onion flakes and salad dressing. Drizzle with hot sauce and you're ready to eat.

Beef Tips & Rice

Ingredients: 2 (1.3 oz) jalapeno peppers   1 (8 oz) pkg beef tips
1 pkg beef Ramen seasoning   ½ (8 oz) bag rice
2 tbsps squeeze cheese   1 tsp garlic powder
½ tsp coriander & annatto 1 cup hot water
2 tbsps BBQ sauce   1 tbsp butter

Directions: Cut up jalapeno peppers and put all in a clean chip bag. Set the butter aside until the end. Add the rest of the ingredients in a chip bag and stir well. Place the bag in a hot pot and heat for 3 hours. Do not let it dry out. Might need to add a little water to it as it heats. When done, pour all into a spread bowl, add butter, and stir well. Great to eat with buttered bread or a few saltine crackers.

Beef and Dumplings

Ingredients: 1 (11.25 oz) pkg BBQ beef   2 (8 oz) pkgs beef tips
1 (12 oz) V-8 juice   ½ tsp garlic powder
1 (3 oz) beef Ramen noodles (not crushed)
1 pkg beef Ramen seasoning
1 (4 oz) serving green beans
1 (4 oz) serving carrots   1 tbsp onion flakes
½ cup hot water   6 flour tortillas

Directions: Open BBQ beef package and remove all beef pieces. Set BBQ sauce aside. In a chip bag combine all beef tips, beef pieces, V-8 juice, garlic powder, beef Ramen noodles, beef Ramen seasoning, green beans, carrots, onion flakes, and hot water. Place the bag in a hot pot to cook for 2 hours. Tear the flour tortillas into 4 pieces each. Roll the pieces into balls and add to the bag. Put back in hot pot and cook for an additional 1 ½ hours. Stir lightly occasionally. When this is done, you can make up a package of instant potatoes and pour BBQ sauce over top. What an awesome meal this is.

Now That's Spaghetti

Ingredients: 1 (5 oz) summer sausage   2 (1.3 oz) jalapeno peppers
6 (3 oz) chili Ramen noodles
1 heaping tsp black pepper
½ (10 oz) bag cheese puffs   1 (11.25 oz) pkg chili no beans
1 (12 oz) V-8 juice and ½ can water
2 heaping tbsps onion flakes
1 heaping tbsp garlic powder
2/3 (13.5 oz) bottle ketchup

Directions: Grab a large chip bag. Cut summer sausage into small pieces and cut up jalapeno peppers as well. Set your noodles, black pepper, and cheese puffs aside. Combine the rest of the ingredients, stir well, and place in a hot pot to cook for 4 hours. Heat water in a second hot pot and just before sauce is ready, bust up noodles. Get three spread bowls and put two packages of noodles in each bowl. Cook noodles and drain any water. Add black pepper to noodles and stir. Pour the spaghetti sauce over each bowl and stir well. Crush the cheese puffs and divide into each bowl. Stir and get ready to grub. Eat this dish as is or serve with saltine crackers, bread, or tortilla chips.

Just Like Home Spaghetti

Ingredients: 2 (8 oz) pkgs Mexican/ground beef
¼ (13.5 oz) bottle ketchup   2 sweeteners
3 (3 oz) beef Ramen noodles   pepper to taste
4 pieces bread   butter to taste

Directions: In a clean chip bag combine both meat packages, ketchup, and sweeteners. Place bag in a hot pot to heat for 3 hours. The hotter the pot, the better. When ready, cook the noodles and drain water. Pour meat mixture into a spread bowl and add noodles. Stir very well. Add pepper, and you're ready to eat. Butter bread, if available, and eat up. Might need to invite a friend unless you are really hungry.

Cheeseburger Helper

Ingredients: 2 (3 oz) beef Ramen noodles
½ (5 oz) summer sausage
1 (8 oz) pkg Mexican beef   2 pkgs beef Ramen seasoning
1 tsp onion flakes   ¼ bottle squeeze cheese
1 (1.5 oz) pkg ranch dressing   4 pieces bread
1 tbsp butter (if available)

Directions: Leave noodles whole and cook in a spread bowl without seasoning. After you cook, add cold water and stir to rinse off starch. Drain when done. Cut summer sausage into small pieces. In a large chip bag combine Mexican beef, Ramen noodles, Ramen seasoning packages, onion flakes, summer sausage, cheese, and ranch dressing. Mix well and place in a hot pot to cook for 2 hours. Once done, put in a spread bowl, butter the bread, and dig in. You will be good and full.

Sweet Ole' Pot Roast

Ingredients: 2 (1.3 oz) jalapeno peppers
1 (11.25 oz) pkg pot roast   2 ½ tbsps squeeze cheese
½ (8 oz) bag rice   1 tbsp habanera sauce
1 (12 oz) orange juice
pinch salt and pepper to taste
1 (8 oz) pkg Mexican ground beef

Directions: Chop up both jalapeno peppers into small pieces and take out seeds. Mix all ingredients, except cheese, in a large chip bag. Place bag into hot pot and cook for 1 ½ hours, stirring occasionally. Pour this into the spread bowl and top with cheese. You will not believe the taste. Great poured over instant potatoes. Eat with buttered bread or flour tortillas.

Pot Roast Perfection

Ingredients: 1 (1.3 oz) jalapeno pepper   ¼ (8 oz) bag rice
1 (12 oz) V-8/Tomato juice
1 (11.25 oz) pkg pot roast
2 tbsps squeeze cheese   ¼ cup water
1 (4 oz) pkg instant potato flakes (any flavor)

Directions: Cut up jalapeno pepper and put in a large chip bag. Add rice, V-8/Tomato juice, and pot roast to the bag. Place this in a hot pot to cook for 30 minutes. Now, add the squeeze cheese and ¼ cup water. Leave in the hot pot for another hour. Just before you remove the mixture from the hot pot, cook the instant potatoes in a spread bowl with just enough water to hydrate. Once potatoes are done, put in a pile in the center of the bowl. Remove bag from hot pot and pour over the top of the potatoes. Simply delicious.

Sheppard's Pie

Ingredients: 1 (4 oz) pkg instant potato flakes (any flavor)
1 (4 oz) serving corn   1 (8 oz) pkg Mexican beef
½ tsp onion powder   1 (4 oz) serving green beans
½ tsp garlic powder   3 tbsps squeeze cheese
1 tsp habanera sauce   Salt and pepper to taste

Directions: In a spread bowl cook the instant potatoes per directions.
Place in a large chip bag when done. Now add all ingredients to the chip bag
and knead well. Place the bag in a hot pot to cook for 3 to 4 hours. When
done, place all in a spread bowl and top with salt and pepper. Can also add
some summer sausage, if you desire. This is a very good meal.

Chicken Dishes

Orange Chicken With Sweet & Spicy Glaze

Ingredients:
- 2 (1.3 oz) jalapeno peppers
- 1 (12 oz) pineapple orange juice
- 2 pkgs sweetener   1 fireball (crushed)
- 1 (7 oz) pkg chicken chunks
- 2 tbsps salad dressing   1 tsp habanera sauce
- squeeze cheese to taste
- 1 (3 oz) chicken Ramen noodles
- 1 (3 oz) chili Ramen noodles
- 1 (2 oz) pkg hot peanuts   1 pkg chicken Ramen seasoning

Directions: Cut up jalapeno peppers and set aside. Using your insert cup combine 6 tbsps of pineapple orange juice, 1 sweetener, jalapeno peppers, and the crushed fireball. Set cup aside while preparing the rest. Open the chicken chunks package and add 1 sweetener and enough juice to cover meat. Marinade for 2 to 3 hours. After chicken chunks marinade, place package in a hot pot and heat for 1 hour. Right before you pull package out of hot pot, add salad dressing and habanera sauce to insert cup, with a good shot of cheese. Stir well. Remove chicken chunks from hot pot and place insert cup in hot pot for 10 minutes. Mixture should be creamy.

While it heats, use a chip bag and combine both noodle packages, half the chili Ramen seasoning package, and the rest of the juice. Cover the rest of the way with hot water and knead all well. Tie up and wrap bag in a towel and let cook. Once all is done, drain juice from bag and pour noodles in spread bowl. Stir in all the contents of chicken chunks package as well as the contents of the insert cup. Coat the top of meal with hot peanuts and cover with chicken Ramen seasoning package. Hope you are really hungry.

Tahitian Chicken

Ingredients:
1 (7 oz) pkg chicken chunks/chicken quarter
1/3 onion or 2 tbsps onion flakes
2 tbsps homemade soy sauce
1 (12 oz) pineapple orange juice
¼ cup brown sugar
1 (4 oz) serving pineapple chunks from tray
2 tbsps cornstarch   ¼ cup melted butter
1 (2 oz) pkg energy mix

Directions: Shred chicken and cut up onion, if available. Make the soy sauce from recipe in book. Mix until all is dissolved. Use a clean chip bag and combine all ingredients listed above, except the energy mix. Marinade in the bag for 4 hours. Now place the bag in a hot pot and cook for 3 hours. Stir occasionally. When done, drain juice, pour chicken mixture in a spread bowl, add energy mix, and stir well. Dig in. It is time for a real treat. Left over juices can be poured over rice. You can use some energy mix in rice as well. As you can see, you need a little help from the kitchen.

Lemon-Pepper Chicken

Ingredients:
12 pieces lemon candy   2 tbsps hot water
1 (.34 oz) pkg lemon lime sports drink mix/lemon cooloff
1 (7 oz) pkg chicken chunks   ½ (8 oz) bag rice
1 (12 oz) Sprite   pepper to taste

Directions: Break candies into small pieces and put in your insert cup. Add a shot of hot water to melt candies. Stir in sports drink mix/cooloff, add another shot of hot water, and mix well. Drain juice from chicken chunks into insert cup and stir. Place insert in a hot pot and heat for 2 hours. In a clean chip bag combine rice, Sprite, and chicken chunks and place in another hot pot to cook for the same 2 hours. When all is ready, you can pour off juice in chip bag, pour mixture into a spread bowl, and stir in candy mixture. Top off with a little pepper. Grab your favorite drink and eat up. Really good!

Sweet & Sour Chicken & Rice

Ingredients:
    1 (7 oz) pkg chicken chunks
    1 (12 oz) pineapple orange juice
    2 pkgs sweetener   2 ½ tsps pickle juice
    1 (1.3 oz) jalapeno pepper (chopped)
    ½ (8 oz) bag rice

Directions: Drain and shred chicken chunks. In a large chip bag combine chicken chunks, pineapple orange juice, sweeteners, pickle juice, and chopped jalapeno pepper. Place bag in a hot pot to heat and marinade for 4 hours. Remove bag and add rice to mixture. Place back in hot pot for another 45 minutes. Might need to add a little water. MMM good! If no pineapple orange juice is available, use a regular orange juice.

Chicken & Dumplings

Ingredients:
    1 (7 oz) pkg chicken chunks   1 tsp pepper
    2 pkgs chicken Ramen seasoning   1 tsp onion powder
    1 tbsp onion flakes   1/2 tbsp garlic powder
    1 (3 oz) chicken Ramen noodles
    3 tbsps starch if available   1 (4 oz) serving green beans
    2 (4 oz) servings carrots   1 heaping shot squeeze cheese
    ¼ (3.2 oz) bag instant milk   1 ½ cups hot water
    6 flour tortillas

Directions: In a large chip bag combine all the ingredients except the flour tortillas. Mix well. Tear tortillas into quarters and roll into balls. Add them to bag. Cook for 3 ½ hours. Best to double bag the meal. If meal becomes dry while cooking, then add enough water to keep thick and creamy.

Chicken Spaghetti

Ingredients: 2 (3 oz) chicken Ramen noodles
2 pkgs chicken Ramen seasoning
1 light tsp garlic powder   2 tbsps salsa/picante sauce
1 (13.5 oz) ketchup   1 (12 oz) V-8 juice
1 (7 oz) pkg chicken chunks

Directions: Put both packages of noodles (do not crush) in a spread bowl for a moment. Using a clean chip bag combine both Ramen seasoning packages with the rest of the ingredients. Mix well. Place the mixture in a hot pot to cook for 6 hours. About 30 minutes before sauce is ready, add Ramen noodles to bag without busting up too much. Leave all in the hot pot for remaining 30 minutes. Remove from hot pot, pour into a spread bowl, and eat up. Great meal for a very hungry person.

Chicken Salad

Ingredients: 1 tbsp onion flakes   ¼ (9 oz) dill pickle
1 heaping tbsp relish   1 tsp pepper
1 (7 oz) pkg chicken chunks   2 tbsps salad dressing
1 pkg chicken Ramen seasoning   3 boiled eggs

Directions: Using a little hot water, hydrate the onion flakes. In a spread bowl, cut up pickle and add relish, pepper, chicken chunks, salad dressing, and chicken Ramen seasoning package and mix well. Now cut up eggs into fairly small pieces and stir into mixture. Serve on bread, crackers, or tortilla chips.

BBQ Chicken

Ingredients: 1 (7 oz) pkg chicken chunks
2 tbsps hot sauce   1tbsp onion flakes
¼ (18 oz) bottle BBQ sauce   ½ tsp garlic powder

Directions: Rinse off chicken chunks package and open. Pour in all ingredients to this package and place in a hot pot to heat for 3 hours. Remove and serve. This is great with a side dish of mashed potatoes and sweet & sour rice.

Chicken-Chili Nachos

Ingredients: 2 (11.25 oz) pkgs chicken chili
               2 (1.3 oz) jalapeno peppers
               1 (6 oz) bag salsa Verde chips
               ½ (12 oz) bag refried beans
               ¼ (16 oz) bottle squeeze cheese
               1 (16 oz) bag tortilla chips

Directions: Rinse off chicken chili meat packages and place in a hot pot to heat. Cut up the jalapeno peppers and crush salsa Verde chips. In a spread bowl cook the refried beans. When meat packs are hot, pour into refried beans and add squeeze cheese and salsa Verde chips. Stir well. Using a separate spread bowl, layer bowl with tortilla chips, half mixture and half the jalapeno peppers. Repeat these steps a second time. You can top off with hot sauce if you like it extra hot and spicy.

Cheesy Chicken Burritos

Ingredients: 1 (7 oz) pkg chicken chunks   ½ (8 oz) bag rice
               1 (8 oz) bag jalapeno chips
               ¼ (16 oz) bottle squeeze cheese
               1 pkg chicken Ramen seasoning
               2 cups hot water   6 flour tortillas

Directions: Drain and shred chicken chunks. In your spread bowl cook rice as directed. Crush the jalapeno chips. To the chip bag, add rice, chicken chunks, squeeze cheese, and Ramen seasoning package. Add a little hot water, enough to hydrate chips. Place chip bag in a hot pot and heat for 30 minutes. When done, roll up in the flour tortillas. Put all in a clean chip bag and put back in a hot pot for 30 more minutes. Add toppings if you desire. Great with some party mix and cold drink.

Mexican Dishes

Tasty Tostitos

Ingredients: 2 (1.3 oz) jalapeno peppers 5 (.75 oz) pkgs cream cheese
1 (8 oz) pkg Mexican beef ¼ (12 oz) bottle salsa
1 (16 oz) bag corn chips

Directions: Cut up jalapeno peppers. In a spread bowl, combine cream cheese, Mexican beef, jalapeno peppers, and salsa and mix well. Crush the corn chips in the chip bag and add enough hot water to knead. You do not want this too wet. Just moist so that chips stick together. Once kneaded, flatten out in bag and cut open. Now use a clean, full soda can, and roll out until mixture is thin. Cut up mixture with ID card into squares about 6" x 8". Spoon a little mixture into dough and roll up. Put them in a chip bag and place in a hot pot to heat for 2 ½ hours. Can top with cheese if you desire, but it is up to you. This is also good with chicken chunks. Do not be afraid to be creative.

Texas-Penn Tamales

Ingredients: 2 (8 oz) pkgs Mexican beef ¼ (12 oz) bag refried beans
1 (12 oz) V-8 juice 1 (27.2 oz) pkg flour tortillas
½ (16 oz) bottle squeeze cheese ½ (12 oz) bottle salsa

Directions: In a clean chip bag combine the Mexican beef package as well as the refried beans. Add half the can of V-8 juice and place in a hot pot for 1 hour. Separate the flour tortillas and lightly spread some cheese on each. Remove mixture from hot pot and spoon onto each tortilla. Do not make too thick. Roll them up, put about 6 in a clean chip bag, and place in the hot pot for 45 minutes. Remove, place in a spread bowl, and top with salsa. You can add some jalapeno peppers if you wish, but these are plenty good as they are.

The Ultimate Burritos

Ingredients: 3 (1.3 oz) jalapeno peppers   1 (6 oz) bag salsa Verde chips
2 (1.75 oz) bags pork skins (small)
3 (11.25 oz) pkgs chili no beans
2 (11.25 oz) pkgs pot roast   2 pkgs chili Ramen seasoning
½ (16 oz) bottle squeeze cheese
1 (12 oz) spicy/reg V-8 juice
1 (12 oz) bag refried beans   hot water
1 (27.2 oz) pkg flour tortillas
½ (10 oz) bag cheese puffs

You will need: 4 hot pots

Directions: Cut up the jalapeno peppers and crush the salsa Verde chips and pork skins. In a clean chip bag, combine the jalapeno peppers, crushed chips, pork skins, 2 chili no beans, both pot roasts, both chili Ramen seasoning packages, ¼ bottle squeeze cheese, V-8 juice, refried beans, and 1/3 cup of hot water. Knead together very well. Separate the flour tortillas and divide mixture between all. Roll all up in burritos and place 4 in a small chip bag. Repeat this until all are in bags. Place each bag in a hot pot and cook for 2 hours. When done, grab 3 spread bowls and place 4 burritos in each bowl. Cut open last chili no beans and pour 1/3 in each bowl over burritos. Crush the cheese puffs and top off the burritos. You can choose to use some habanera sauce, but you really do not need to.

Loaded and Coated Burritos

Ingredients: ½ cup rice   ½ cup refried beans
1 (11.25 oz) pkg chili with beans
2 (1.3 oz) jalapeno peppers
1 handful jalapeno chips   8 flour tortillas

squeeze cheese to taste   1 (1.5 oz) pkg ranch dressing
1 cup cheese puffs   habanera sauce to taste
hot water

You will need: 2 spread bowls

Directions: In a spread bowl combine rice and refried beans and cook. While waiting, rinse the meat package and place in a hot pot to heat. Cut up your jalapeno peppers and crush the jalapeno chips. When meat package is good and hot, pour it into the beans and rice and stir well. Add the jalapeno peppers and chips and stir again. Separate the flour tortillas and coat each with some squeeze cheese. Spoon the mixture onto tortillas and roll up. Take 4 and place them in a small chip bag. Repeat this with the other 4. Place them in 2 separate hot pots to heat for 2 hours. When done, place 4 burritos in 2 separate bowls and cover with ranch dressing. Crush up the cheese puffs and coat both bowls. Can drizzle with habanera sauce now. They will be pretty spicy. You are in for a real treat. Enjoy!

Seg-Soft Tacos

Ingredients: 4 flour tortillas   3 tbsps squeeze cheese
2 (1.3 oz) jalapeno peppers
1 (8 oz) serving ground beef from tray
1 (4 oz) serving of corn from tray
1 pkg beef/chili Ramen seasoning
2 (.75 oz) pkgs cream cheese   ¼ (12 oz) bottle salsa

Directions: Separate the flour tortillas and coat with a layer of squeeze cheese. Cut up the jalapeno peppers. In a spread bowl, combine the ground beef, corn, jalapeno peppers, and the Ramen seasoning package. Stir well and spoon onto 4 flour tortillas. Top each off with a ½ package cream cheese and fold over into your taco. Put all 4 in a clean chip bag and place in a hot pot to heat for 1 ½ hours. When done, put the tacos in a spread bowl and pour the salsa over the top. Eat em' up.

Insider Burladas

Ingredients: 5 (11.25 oz) pkgs chili no beans

2 (11.25 oz) pkgs chili with beans
1 (8 oz) pkg Mexican/ground beef
1 (12 oz) bag refried beans   ½ (8 oz) bag jalapeno chips
1 (18 oz) box cheese nips   ½ (1.75 oz) bag pork skins
2 (27.2 oz) pkgs flour tortillas
1 (15 oz) bottle chili con queso
6 (1.3 oz) jalapeno peppers   1 (12 oz) bottle salsa

You will need: 3 hot pots

Directions: Rinse all meat packages and place in hot pots to heat. In a spread bowl cook the refried beans while meat packages heat. In a separate spread bowl crush up jalapeno chips and cheese nips. Spoon in 3 to 4 tbsps of water to start. Slowly add 1 ½ tbsps and stir until you create a paste. Remove Mexican/ground beef and chili with beans from hot pots and pour into refried beans. Crush pork skins and stir into mixture. Separate the flour tortillas and coat each with some paste mixture and chili con queso. Spoon the bean mixture onto the tortillas and roll them up. Get several chip bags now. Place 4 to 5 burritos in each bag. Place bags in the hot pots to heat for 2 ½ to 3 hours. Right before you remove all from hot pots, cut up the jalapeno peppers. Now grab 5 spread bowls and put 4 burritos in each bowl. Cover them with the chili without beans meat packages. Drizzle each bowl with more chili con queso and decorate with the jalapeno peppers. This will feed 5 hungry men for sure. Burrito + Enchilada = Burladas. If cheese nips are not available, you can use cheese puffs. Top off bowls with salsa. The real belt buster.

Tasty Tacos

Ingredients: 2 (1.3 oz) jalapeno peppers
1 (8 oz) bag reg potato chips
¼ (12 oz) bag refried beans   1 (3 oz) small bag Cheetos
1 pkg chili Ramen seasoning   1 (8 oz) pkg beef tips
¼ cup hot water   squeeze cheese to taste
habanera sauce to taste   1 (27.2 oz) pkg flour tortillas

Directions: Cut up the jalapeno peppers and crush the chips. In a clean chip bag combine all ingredients, except the flour tortillas. Mix well and place in a hot pot to heat for 45 minutes. Remove this from hot pot and spoon the mixture on the flour tortillas and fold in half. Carefully place 3 to 4 in a clean chip bag and place in a hot pot to heat for 1 full hour. Repeat until all are cooked. When ready, remove from hot pot and grab a drink. Can also make a side of rice. This will be one to enjoy.

Nachos #1

Ingredients: 1 (11.25 oz) pkg chili no beans
1 (11.25 oz) pkg chili with beans
1 (3 oz) chili Ramen noodles   ½ (12 oz) bag refried beans
1 (9 oz) pickle reg or hot   6 (1.3 oz) jalapeno peppers
1 (16 oz) bag tortilla chips   ½ (16 oz) bottle squeeze cheese
1 (1.5 oz) pkg ranch dressing   hot sauce to taste

Directions: Rinse both meat packages and put in a hot pot to heat. While they heat, cook the soup and refried beans together in a spread bowl. Cut up the pickle and the jalapeno peppers and set aside. When meat packages are hot, pour into bean mixture and stir well. In a separate spread bowl, layer bowl with tortilla chips and top with bean mixture, squeeze cheese, pickles, and jalapeno peppers. Repeat this process until the mixture is gone. Top off with ranch dressing and hot sauce. Hope you're hungry.

Nachos #2

Ingredients: 2 (11.25 oz) pkgs chili with beans
½ (12 oz) bag refried beans
2 (1.3 oz) jalapeno peppers   1 (16 oz) bag tortilla chips
2 (3 oz) bags nacho chips   1 (1.5 oz) pkg ranch dressing
½ (16 oz) bottle squeeze cheese   2 tbsps pickle juice

Directions: Rinse the meat packages and put in a hot pot to heat. In a spread bowl cook the refried beans. Cut up the jalapeno peppers as you wait. When meat packages are hot, pour into the refried beans and stir well. Layer another spread bowl with tortilla chips and nacho chips. Cover with bean mixture. Repeat this process until mixture is gone. Top off with ranch dressing, cheese, and pickle juice. You cannot eat just one.

Hearty Nachos

Ingredients:
    1 (8 oz) pkg Mexican/ground beef
    ¼ (12 oz) bottle salsa
    ¼ (16 oz) bottle squeeze cheese
    3 (1.3 oz) jalapeno peppers
    ¼ (16 oz) bag tortilla chips

Directions: Rinse meat package and open. Add the salsa and cheese and put in a hot pot. Cut up the jalapeno peppers while heating. Allow meat package to heat for 1 hour. Layer a spread bowl with tortilla chips and pour meat package over the top. Decorate with jalapeno peppers. Quick snack to enjoy on a rainy day.

Fabulous Frito Pie

Ingredients:
    1 (16 oz) bag corn chips   ¼ (12 oz) bag refried beans
    1 (11.25 oz) pkg chili no beans
    2 (8 oz) pkgs Mexican beef   ¼ (12 oz) bottle salsa
    ¼ (3 oz) bottle onion flakes
    3 (1.3 oz) jalapeno peppers   ¼ (3.5 oz) pkg pepperoni slices
    ½ (16 oz) bag tortilla chips   3 (.75 oz) pkgs cream cheese
    ¼ (16 oz) bottle squeeze cheese
    1 (1.5 oz) pkg ranch dressing

Directions: Crush up corn chips in bag and add just enough hot water so that the mixture sticks together. Knead into a dough. Put it in a spread bowl and work dough into a pie crust. Smooth when done. Place bowl under a fan to dry for 2 hours. While crust is drying, place refried beans, chili no beans, the Mexican beef, salsa, and onion flakes in a chip bag with ¼ cup water and place in a hot pot to heat while the crust dries. Cut up the jalapeno peppers and the pepperoni slices. Lightly crush tortilla chips. When crust is dry, remove bean mixture from hot pot. Take the 3 packages of cream cheese and coat the entire crust. Spoon in half the bean mixture, half the tortilla chips, half the peppers, and half the pepperoni slices. Top with squeeze cheese. Now repeat this process again and once done pour ranch dressing over the top. Let sit for 30 minutes. Can cut just like a pie and serve. This is just fabulous.

Killer Frito Pie

Ingredients:
1 (11.5 oz) pkg chili with beans
½ (16 oz) squeeze cheese to taste
¼ (5 oz) bottle habanero sauce
3 (1.3 oz) jalapeno peppers
½ (12 oz) bag refried beans   1 (16 oz) bag corn chips

Directions: Rinse the package of chili and place in a hot pot to heat for 20 minutes. Open package and add a shot of cheese and a tbsp of habanero sauce. Stir well and add 3 tsps water. Stir and put back in hot pot for another 30 minutes. While it heats, cut up all peppers and add to package. In a spread bowl, pour in refried beans and add enough hot water to cook. When meat package is finished heating, pour into refried beans, with the remaining cheese and habanero sauce and stir well. In another spread bowl add 1/3 bag of chips and top with bean mixture. Repeat this step until all are gone. Grab your favorite drink and relax. It is time to eat.

My Menudo #1

Ingredients:
¼ (16 oz) bag tortilla chips   ¼ (8 oz) bag rice
1 (5 oz) summer sausage (or use spam as substitute)
1 (11.25 oz) pkg chili no beans
2 pkgs chili Ramen seasoning
3 (1.75 oz) bags pork skins
½ (9 oz) pickle (reg or hot)   3 tbsps pickle juice

Directions: Crush the tortilla chips and put in a spread bowl. In a separate spread bowl cook the rice. Once rice is cooked, add the chips to the bowl with 1 cup hot water. Knead it into a dough. Once kneaded, place dough in a clean chip bag and place in a hot pot for 20 minutes. Cut up the summer sausage or spam into small pieces and in a separate spread bowl combine the sausage/spam, the chili no beans, 2 chili Ramen seasoning packages, and 1 cup hot water. Cover for a moment. Combine the pork skins and 1 cup hot water in another bowl. Once pork skins are soft, combine both bowls and the bag of rice. Mix all well. Now stir in the pickles and the pickle juice. Serve it up.

Maryland Manudo

Ingredients:
- ½ (8 oz) bag rice
- 2 cups hot water
- 1 (9 oz) reg or hot pickle
- 3 tbsps onion flakes
- 3 (1.75 oz) bags pork skins
- 3 tbsps pickle juice
- 3 (4 oz) servings mixed vegetables
- 1 (4 oz) serving corn
- 1 cup crushed tortilla chips
- 1 (3 oz) pkg spam
- 1 (12 oz) can V-8 juice
- 1 tbsp garlic powder
- 2 tbsps hot sauce
- 2 pkgs beef Ramen seasoning
- 1 (6 oz) pkg corn nuts

You will need: several bowls, 2 hot pots

Directions: In one spread bowl cook the rice. While rice is cooking, in a separate spread bowl, combine crushed tortilla chips with 1/3 cup of hot water and knead into a dough like substance. When the rice is done, add it to the dough and knead again. Place this mixture into a chip bag and place in a hot pot and heat for 30 minutes. While it is heating, cut up spam and pickle. In a spread bowl combine the spam, pickle, V-8 juice, onion flakes, and garlic powder. Mix well. Pour this mixture into another chip bag and place in the other hot pot to heat for 20 to 30 minutes. While both are heating, place the pork skins in a spread bowl and add just enough water to hydrate all. Once completed, combine the mixtures, the pork skins, and the rest of the ingredients and mix well. Top off bowl with the corn nuts if available.

My Gumbo

Ingredients:
- 1 (5 oz) summer sausage
- 1 (7 oz) pkg chicken chunks
- ½ (1.75 oz) bag pork skins
- 1 (12 oz) can V-8 juice
- ¼ (8 oz) bag rice
- 1 (3.5 oz) pkg mackerel
- 2 (1.3 oz) jalapeno peppers
- 1 pkg chili Ramen seasoning

Directions: Cut summer sausage into small pieces. Drain mackerel and chicken chunks. Break up meat packages and combine all in a spread bowl. Crush up pork skins and cut up jalapeno peppers. Add the rest of the ingredients with a cup of hot water. Pour mixture into a large chip bag and shake well. Place this bag in a hot pot to cook for 4 hours. What a great meal this is.

Spam Dishes, & Ham

Cellblock Cookin's Ham-Mac & Cheese

Ingredients:
1 (1.3 oz) jalapeno pepper   2 (3 oz) pkgs spam
1 (3 oz) chicken Ramen noodles   ½ tsp salt
1 tsp black pepper   1 pkg chicken Ramen seasoning
½ cup squeeze cheese   ¼ cup salad dressing
½ sleeve crackers

Directions: Cut the jalapeno pepper and spam into fairly small pieces. In a spread bowl cook the Ramen noodles. When cooked, drain and rinse the noodles. Add the salt, pepper, Ramen seasoning package, squeeze cheese, and salad dressing. Stir well, then add the jalapeno pepper pieces and spam. Stir again. If you want it cheesier, add another shot of cheese. Look out Kraft, you have some competition. Perfect meal for one. Eat on tortilla chips or with crackers.

Pineapple, Spam & Rice

Ingredients:
¼ (8 oz) bag rice   1 (3 oz) pkg spam
1 filling from (4 oz) cherry pie
1 (4 oz) serving pineapples from tray

Directions: In a spread bowl cook rice. Cut spam into pieces and separate cherry filling from pie. Drain all juices from pineapples. (If you like, you can drink the juice) Combine all the ingredients in a clean chip bag, place in a hot pot, and heat for 1 ½ to 2 hours. Pour all in a spread bowl when done and eat up. Just like home.

Spam Salad

Ingredients: 1 (3 oz) pkg spam/ham   2 hard boiled eggs
                 1 tsp onion flakes   ¼ (9 oz) pickle (reg/hot)
                 ½ tsp relish   1 heaping tbsp salad dressing
                 ¼ tsp black pepper   ¼ tsp garlic powder

Directions: Cut spam/ham into fairly small pieces. Cut eggs into pieces as well. Set the eggs aside until the end. Hydrate the onion flakes in a little hot water. Mix all the ingredients and stir well. Add eggs and lightly stir again. You can eat this on bread, tortilla chips, or saltine crackers. Do not be afraid to add a shot of squeeze cheese.

Spam and Cheese Sandwich

Ingredients: 2 tbsps squeeze cheese   1 tsp salad dressing
                 ¼ (9 oz) pickle (reg/hot)   2 pieces bread
                 1 (3 oz) pkg spam

Directions: Spread cheese and salad dressing on bread. Cut the pickle into slices and add to bread. Open the package of spam and line all on the bread. You can eat this hot or cold. To heat, place sandwich in a small chip bag and place in a hot pot to heat for about 30 to 45 minutes. Grab your favorite chips and drink and enjoy your meal.

Spam Cheeseburgers

Ingredients: 2 (1.3 oz) jalapeno peppers   ½ (9 oz) pickle
                 ½ (10 oz) bag cheese puffs   1 (3 oz) pkg spam
                 6 pieces bread   salt to taste

pepper to taste   salad dressing to taste

Directions: Cut jalapeno peppers and pickle into small pieces. Crush the cheese puffs and dice up spam. In a spread bowl combine spam, cheese puffs, jalapeno peppers, and pickle and knead well. Divide mixture into 3 equal parts and form patties. Use 3 small chip bags and place a patty in each bag. Place the bags in a hot pot to heat for 2 hours. When cook time has expired remove patties. Put each patty on bread and top with salt, pepper, and salad dressing. Break out your favorite chips and drink.

Slice of Seafood Pizza

Ingredients:
  1 (16 oz) bag corn chips   ¼ (12 oz) bag refried beans
  1 (12 oz) V-8 juice   2 (3.5 oz) pkgs mackerel
  1 (7 oz) pkg chicken chunks   1 (4.23) pkg tuna
  ½ (3.5 oz) pkg (25 pcs) pepperoni slices
  2 (1.3 oz) jalapeno peppers
  1 (13.5 oz) bottle ketchup
  1 pkg Ramen shrimp seasoning
  1 tsp onion powder   1 tsp garlic powder
  ¼ (3 oz) bottle onion flakes 1 ½ tbsps habanera sauce
  ½ (16 oz) bottle squeeze cheese   1 (3.53 oz) pkg sardines
  ½ (11 oz) bag party mix   ½ (9 oz) pickle
You will need: rice bag, newspaper, 2 hot pots

Directions: Prepare the crust. Crush the corn chips into a fine powder.
Add refried beans to the corn chip bag with about 1/3 cup hot water. Knead
into a pliable dough. Might need to add a tbsp or 2 of water as you knead.
Flatten this out in the bag, wrap in newspaper, and set aside. While this sets
up, prepare the sauce.
      Prepare sauce. In rice bag combine V-8 juice, 1 package mackerel,
chicken chunks, tuna, pepperoni slices, 2 diced jalapeno peppers, ketchup,

shrimp Ramen seasoning, onion powder, garlic powder, onion flakes, and the habanero sauce. Stir bag well and place in a hot pot to heat for 3 ½ hours.

Once all is ready, cut open chip bag and flatten out pizza until it is fairly thin. Pour cheese on top of it and spread evenly. Remove sauce from pot and pour sauce over pizza. Crush party mix and open sardines. Decorate pizza with sardines, party mix, and pickle. Can use more cheese if you desire.

Meat Lover's Pizza

Ingredients: 1 (5 oz) summer sausage
1 (8 oz) pkg Mexican/ground beef
1 (11.25 oz) pkg chili no beans
4 (3 oz) chili Ramen noodles   ½ (16 oz) bag corn chips
½ (12 oz) bag refried beans 2 pkgs chili Ramen seasoning
1 (9 oz) pickle (reg/hot)   4 (1.3 oz) jalapeno peppers
½ (8 oz) bag jalapeno chips ½ (16 oz) bottle squeeze cheese
¼ (13.5 oz) bottle ketchup   hot sauce to taste
You will need: 2 hot pots, newspaper

Directions: Cut the summer sausage into small pieces. Rinse all meat packages. Put all pieces of summer sausage into meat packages and place all in a hot pot to heat for 1 hour. While these heat, crush up Ramen noodles, corn chips, and combine in a large chip bag. Shake well. Now, add the refried beans and Ramen seasoning packages and shake again. Pour in enough hot water to be absorbed and cook all. Do not flood. Flatten and even this out in the chip bag. Wrap in newspaper when done and set aside for 15 minutes. While you wait, cut up pickle and jalapeno peppers and crush jalapeno chips. Unwrap pizza, cut open bag, and cover with a layer of cheese. Remove meat packages from hot pot and evenly spread all over pizza. Pile on the pickles, jalapeno peppers, and jalapeno chips. Now, you can drizzle with the ketchup. Top off with hot sauce, cut, and serve.

Hawaiian Pizza

Ingredients: 2 (11.25 oz) pkgs chili with beans

2 (8 oz) cups fruit cocktail juice from tray*
4 (3 oz) Ramen noodles (any flavor)
½ (12 oz) bag refried beans   4 (1.3 oz) jalapeno peppers
1 (9 oz) pickle   ¼ (16 oz) bag corn chips
½ (16 oz) bottle squeeze cheese
1 (8 oz) cup of fruit cocktail*   habanera sauce to taste

You will need: 2 hot pots

Directions: Rinse meat packages and place in one hot pot. In a clean chip bag pour both cups of fruit cocktail juice and place in second pot to heat. Now, while waiting, break up all the noodles and put in a chip bag. Add refried beans to bag. Cut up the jalapeno peppers and pickle and set aside. Crush up the corn chips and add to noodles. When fruit juice is hot, pour into bag with Ramen mixture and knead well. Might need to add some hot water to this. Knead the mixture and flatten out evenly in bag. Wrap chip bag in newspaper and set aside for 15 minutes. When ready, unwrap bag and cut open. Cover pizza with cheese and pour hot meat packages over top. Decorate pizza with all fruit, pickles, and jalapeno peppers. Drizzle with habanera sauce. Grab a cold drink and enjoy every bite.
*Ask the kitchen for extra portions to get the required quantities.

Big House Spicy Pizza

Ingredients: 1 (11.25 oz) pkg chili with beans
3 (3 oz) chili Ramen noodles   ¼ (16 oz) bag corn chips
1 (6 oz) bag salsa Verde chips
¼ (12 oz) bag refried beans   ¼ (8 oz) bag rice
1 pkg chili Ramen seasoning
3 (1.3 oz) jalapeno peppers   1 (9 oz) pickle (reg/hot)
¼ (8 oz) bag jalapeno chips   ¼ (14 oz) jar salad dressing
¼ (16 oz) bottle squeeze cheese

You will need: newspaper

Directions: Rinse meat package and place in a hot pot to heat. Crush noodles, corn chips, and salsa Verde chips and combine in a large chip bag. Add refried beans and rice. Shake bag well to mix. Add the Ramen seasoning package and shake again. Pour very hot water into the bag and knead as you do. Do not flood, only enough water to be absorbed. Cook all.

Flatten this out evenly in the chip bag and wrap in newspaper. Set aside for 15 minutes. While waiting, cut up the jalapeno peppers and pickle. Crush the jalapeno chips. When pizza is ready, unwrap pizza and cut open bag. Cover pizza with salad dressing and squeeze cheese. Remove meat package from hot pot and pour over the pizza and even out. Decorate pizza with the jalapeno peppers and pickle and top with jalapeno chips. If you desire, top off with a little ketchup or ranch dressing. Incredibly good meal!!

Player's Pizza

Ingredients:
2 (3.5 oz) pkgs mackerel   2 (11.25 oz) pkgs chili no beans
4 (1.3 oz) jalapeno peppers   ½ (9 oz) hot/reg pickle
2 (5 oz) summer sausages   1 (12 oz) V-8 juice
4 (3 oz) chili Ramen noodles
½ (12 oz) bag refried beans
1 (1.75 oz) bag pork skins (crushed)
1 (6 oz) bag salsa Verde chips (crushed)
1 pkg chili Ramen seasoning
1 (3 oz) bag nacho chips (crushed)
½ (16 oz) bottle squeeze cheese
3 (1.5 oz) pkgs ranch dressing   hot sauce to taste

You will need: small chip bag, a large cheese puffs bag, newspaper, 2 hot pots, and a few bowls

Directions: Rinse all meat packages and place in a hot pot to heat. Cut up the jalapeno peppers, pickle, and summer sausages. Pour V-8 juice into a small chip bag and add summer sausage. Place this in a separate hot pot to heat. After about 1 hour get the cheese puffs bag and combine noodles, refried beans, crushed pork skins, and crushed salsa Verde chips. Drain V-8 juice from summer sausages and pour juice in Ramen mixture. Add enough hot water to cook all. Knead contents until almost all the liquid is absorbed. Flatten bag evenly and wrap in newspaper and set aside. In a spread bowl combine all meat packages with 1 chili Ramen seasoning package. After 15 minutes unwrap pizza and cut bag open. Layer pizza in this way: cheese, meat mixture, summer sausage, pickle and jalapeno pieces, and crushed nacho chips. Once pizza has been decorated nicely, top with ranch dressing and hot sauce. This is a players pizza because only a true player can flip the bill for this one.

My-Hop Pancakes

Ingredients: 1 (.75 oz) pkg cream cheese
2 heaping tbsps strawberry preserves or grape jelly
3 pancakes from breakfast tray

Directions: Combine the cream cheese and the strawberry preserves/grape jelly in a cup or on the tray and mix well. Spread over the top of the pancakes and you are back in the world. Thanks for choosing My-Hop!

More My-Hop Pancakes

Ingredients: 1 (.75 oz) pkg cream cheese   1 heaping tbsp peanut butter
¼ (16 oz) bottle chocolate syrup
3 pancakes from breakfast tray

Directions: In a spread bowl or a cup, combine the first three ingredients and mix well. Spread over the top of the pancakes. This mixture is also good on Ritz crackers. If no chocolate syrup is available, use hot chocolate mix but melt in a hot pot with a little water. Make sure this is fully melted. Just as good.

Creamy Oatmeal

Ingredients: 1 (43 grams) pkg instant oatmeal
                1 tbsp peanut butter   2 oatmeal cream pies

Directions: Cook the oatmeal but leave a little thick. Spoon in the peanut butter and stir well. Break up the oatmeal cream pies, add to bowl, and stir again. Time to enjoy the best oatmeal ever.

Peanut Butter Oatmeal

Ingredients: 2 cups oatmeal (any flavor)
                ½ (3.2 oz) pkg instant milk   3 tbsps peanut butter
                hot water   1 pkg sweetener (2 tsp sugar)
                1 Butterfinger candy bar

Directions: Cook all the oatmeal but leave a little thick. In an insert cup combine instant milk, peanut butter, and sweetener. Stir in 2 tbsps hot water. Place this in a hot pot to melt. Once melted, pour mixture into the oatmeal. Crush up candy bar and top off. Quick, fast, and good!

Breakfast Burritos #1

Ingredients: ¼ (5 oz) summer sausage   2 (1.3 oz) jalapeno peppers
                1/3 (4 oz) pkg instant potato flakes
                2 heaping tbsps refried beans   1 tsp onion flakes
                4 flour tortillas   3 tbsps squeeze cheese
                1 heaping serving scrambled eggs (about 4 eggs)
                ¼ tsp black pepper   1/3 (12 oz) bottle salsa

Directions: Cut up the summer sausage and the jalapeno peppers and set aside. In a spread bowl combine the instant potatoes, refried beans, and onion flakes, with just enough water to cook. Do not want too thin. Separate the flour tortillas and coat with squeeze cheese. Spoon bean mixture onto the tortillas and top with some eggs and summer sausage. Roll up the burritos and place all 4in a small chip bag. Place the bag in a hot pot to cook for 1 hour. When done, remove from hot pot, place in your spread bowl, and top with the salsa and black pepper.

Breakfast Burritos #2

Ingredients: 1 (3.5 oz) pkg mackerel
1 heaping serving scrambled eggs (about 4 eggs)
4 flour tortillas   2 tbsps squeeze cheese
¼ (9 oz) pickle (reg/hot)   2 heaping tbsps refried beans
4 tsps salsa

Directions: Drain juices from mackerel. Place mackerel in a spread bowl and fluff up. Add eggs to bowl and lightly mix. Separate the flour tortillas and coat with some squeeze cheese. Spoon egg mixture into flour tortillas. Cut up the pickle into fairly small pieces and add to burritos. Sprinkle refried beans over all this and roll up. Place all 4 burritos into a small chip bag and place in a hot pot to heat for 1 hour. When they are done, put all in a spread bowl and top with the salsa. You do not have to cook the refried beans. They will cook while in hot pot.

Breakfast Burritos #3

Ingredients: 1 (8 oz) pkg Mexican beef
2 (1.3 oz) jalapeno peppers
1/3 (4 oz) pkg four cheese instant potato flakes
3 tbsps refried beans   2 tsps hot sauce
4 flour tortillas   3 tbsps squeeze cheese
1 heaping serving scrambled eggs (about 4 eggs)
3 tbsps salsa

Directions: Open the package of Mexican beef and rinse well. Cut up the jalapeno peppers and set aside. In a spread bowl, combine instant potatoes, refried beans, and hot sauce. Add just enough water to cook. Not too wet. Separate the flour tortillas and coat with squeeze cheese. Mix together the eggs and Mexican beef in a separate bowl. On each flour tortilla, spoon some of the bean mixture and top with beef mixture. Roll up into burritos and place all four in a small chip bag. Place this bag in a hot pot to heat for 1 hour. When done, remove from hot pot, place all in a spread bowl and top with salsa and jalapeno peppers.

Breakfast Burritos #4

Ingredients: 4 flour tortillas   3 tbsps squeeze cheese
                 1 serving scrambled eggs (about 4 eggs)
                 1 heaping tbsp onion flakes
                 3 heaping tbsps refried beans   4 tbsps salsa

Directions: Separate the flour tortillas and coat each with some squeeze cheese. Combine eggs, onion flakes, and refried beans, and mix well. Spoon the mixture onto the flour tortillas and roll up. Put all 4 in a small chip bag and place in a hot pot to cook for 1 hour. When done, remove from hot pot, place burritos in a spread bowl, and top with salsa.

Cheesy Chicken & Rice

Ingredients:
1 (8 oz) chicken quarter/patty
1 (1.3 oz) jalapeno pepper
1 pkg chicken Ramen seasoning   ¼ (8 oz) bag rice
½ tsp garlic powder   1 tsp onion powder
¼ (16 oz) bottle squeeze cheese   2 tbsps salsa

Directions: Shred chicken quarter or cut up chicken patty. Dice jalapeno pepper. In a chip bag, combine chicken pieces, chicken Ramen seasoning, jalapeno pepper, rice, garlic powder, and onion powder, with 1/3 cup hot water. Place this bag in a hot pot and cook for 2 hours. When ready, pour mixture into a spread bowl, pour in cheese and salsa, stir well and dig in.

Sweet Chicken & Rice

Ingredients:
1 (8 oz) chicken quarter   2 pkgs sweetener
1 (12 oz) orange juice   1 (2 oz) pkg salted peanuts
¼ (2 oz) bag rice   1 pkg chicken Ramen seasoning

Directions: Separate chicken from bone and shred. In a large chip bag combine all ingredients and place in a hot pot to heat for 2 hours. When done, either pour off the juices or leave in. Either way it's just as good.

Pork & Sauerkraut

Ingredients: 3 pork chops (cut into cubes)   1 (3 oz) pkg spam
½ (1.75 oz) bag pork skins 2 (4 oz) servings sauerkraut

Directions: Cut up pork chops and spam. Lightly crush pork skins. Put all ingredients in a large chip bag, with 1/3 cup water. Tie off bag and place in a hot pot for 3 ½ hours. Can add a sprinkle of pepper if you desire. I really love this meal.

Good Ole Cabbage & Ham

Ingredients: 4 (3 oz) pkgs spam/ham
2 (4 oz) servings cabbage
½ pkg shrimp Ramen seasoning

Directions: Cut all spam/ham into cubes. Not too small. Combine all ingredients in a chip bag. Include juices from cabbage, place bag in a hot pot to cook for 6 hours. Pour into a spread bowl and eat up. If you are able to get a tsp. of vinegar, drizzle over dish once done.

Greens & Ham

Ingredients: 2 (3 oz) pkgs ham/spam   1 tbsp onion flakes
1 (4 oz) heaping serving spinach/greens
1 pinch salt & pepper

Directions: Cut up all spam/ham into cubes. Not too small. In a clean chip bag, combine all the ingredients and put it in a hot pot to heat for 1 ½ hours. Pour into a spread bowl and enjoy.

Ad-Seg Goo-Losh

Ingredients: 1 (1.3 oz) jalapeno pepper   4 pieces bread
1 (8 oz) serving chili mac
3 tbsps squeeze cheese   1 (4 oz) serving green beans

2 tbsps hot sauce   1 pinch salt & pepper
1 (4 oz) serving carrots

Directions: Cut up jalapeno pepper and set aside with the bread. Combine the rest of the ingredients in a chip bag and place in a hot pot to heat for 1 hour. Might need to add some water as you heat, but not too much. Remove from the hot pot, butter the bread if possible, and eat until you are full.

Chili Con Corn

Ingredients: 2 (1.3 oz) jalapeno peppers   3 tbsps instant milk
3 tbsps squeeze cheese   1 cup hot water
3 pieces corn bread
1 (4 oz) serving corn   2 (11.25 oz) pkgs chili w/beans
1 (4 oz) serving green beans   1 cup rice

Directions: Cut up jalapeno peppers. Place jalapeno peppers, the instant milk and squeeze cheese in a coffee cup. Fill cup the rest of the way with hot water. Set corn bread aside. Combine all ingredients in a chip bag and place in a hot pot to cook for 4 hours. Might need to add another ¼ cup of water as you heat. When done, pour the mixture into a spread bowl. Crumble up the corn bread and mix in bowl. If you want it spicier, splash with some hot sauce.

Soup Salad

Ingredients: 1 (3 oz) shrimp Ramen noodles
1 (1.3 oz) jalapeno pepper   ¼ (9 oz) pickle (reg/hot)
3 tbsps squeeze cheese
1 (4 oz) serving mixed vegetables 1 tbsp salad dressing
12 tbsps pickle juice   1 tsp pepper
½ tsp garlic powder   ½ tsp onion powder
1 tsp pepper   1 (1.5 oz) pkg ranch dressing

Directions: This is a cold dish. Bust up noodles and cook it a spread bowl. While noodles are cooking, cut up jalapeno pepper and pickle. When noodles have finished cooking, rinse well with cold water. Now, combine all the ingredients, except the ranch dressing, and mix well. Once mixed, pour the ranch dressing over the top. A soup has never been soooo good!!

Hungry Man Hobo

Ingredients: 1 (3 oz) beef Ramen noodles   ½ tsp garlic powder
                ½ tsp onion flakes   ½ tsp onion powder
                1 cup serving ground beef from tray
                1 (4 oz) serving carrots   1 (4 oz) serving green beans
                1 shot habanera sauce   1 shot squeeze cheese
                4 pieces bread

Directions: Cook noodles and beef seasonings from the Ramen noodles, garlic powder, onion flakes, and onion power together while you wait on tray. When tray arrives, add the rest of the ingredients except bread and mix all well. Now butter bread if possible and eat up. Quick, fast, & easy.

Icings

Peanut Butter Cream: 1 package peanut butter cream cookies. Separate cream from cookies and set cookies aside. In a small bowl or cup combine the cookie cream with ½ cup coffee creamer or instant milk. If you use instant milk, add 2 packages sweetener. Add 3 to 4 tbsps of hot water and whip into a thick icing. Whip until smooth and creamy. You can use the cookies to make a pie crust or cake.

Strawberry/Raspberry Cream: 1 package strawberry cream cookies. If strawberry cream cookies are not available, use vanilla cream or Duplex cookies. Mix the cream from the cookies with strawberry Kool-Aid or sports drink. Either way, mix cream from the cookies with 2 cream cheese packages and a tbsp or two of strawberry soda. Follow directions from above with mixing. Once again use cookies for a cake or pie crust.

Vanilla Cream: 1 package vanilla cream cookies or Duplex cream cookies. Separate cream from cookies and set cookies aside. Use water instead of soda, and follow directions with mixtures and ingredients from above.

With the following recipes feel free to add 2 to 3 packages of cream cheese

Cinnamon Icing: 1 package vanilla cream/Duplex cream cookies. Separate cream from cookies and set cookies aside. Crush 10 fireball candies and in an insert cup combine cookie cream, fireballs, and 1 ½ tbsps water. Place this combination in a hot pot to heat and melt for 1 to 1 ½ hours. Stir occasionally. Make sure all is smooth and creamy.

Butterscotch Icing: 1 pkg vanilla cream/Duplex cream cookies. Separate cream from cookies and set cookies aside. Crush half a bag of butterscotch candies, about 25 pieces. In an insert cup combine the crushed candies, cookie cream, and 1 tbsp water. Set the mixture in the hot pot for 1 ½ hours. Stir occasionally.

Lemon Icing: 1 pkg vanilla cream/Duplex cream cookies. Separate cream from cookies and set cookies aside. Crush 25 pieces of lemon candy (can substitute 1 box lemon heads or 1 tbsp lemon Kool Aid from kitchen). In an insert cup combine the lemon flavor, the cookie cream, and 1 tbsp Sprite. Set the mixture in the hot pot for 1 ½ hours. Stir occasionally. Can use 1 tbsp water instead of Sprite, but Sprite is better.

Sticky Sweet Pie Crust

Ingredients: 16 vanilla/peanut butter cream cookies
3 (43 grams) pkgs maple brown sugar oatmeal
1 tsp peanut butter   3 tsps honey

Directions: Separate cream from cookies and set cream aside. Crush cookies as fine as possible. In a spread bowl combine all ingredients except cookie cream with 2 tbsps hot water and knead into a pliable dough. Once kneaded, flatten dough in the bottom of a spread bowl and even out. Starting in the center and using your knuckles, press down and work your way around the bowl towards the outside. Dough will begin to work its way up the sides. Work the dough into a pie crust. Use your hands to smooth the pie crust. When finished, put bowl under a fan for 3 to 4 hours. If your unit has no honey, substitute with a package of syrup from breakfast tray. While crust dries, grab your favorite ingredients to make your filling.

Chocolate Crust

Ingredients: 2 cups hot chocolate mix   1 (3.2 oz) pkg instant milk
1 tbsp peanut butter
3 (43 grams) pkgs regular oatmeal
1 (12 oz) Coca Cola

Directions: In a large spread bowl combine hot chocolate mix, instant milk, peanut butter, oatmeal, and about 4 tbsps of the soda and knead into a thick pliable dough. Might need to add a little more soda but not much. Want just enough to have a moist but not wet dough. Once kneaded, flatten dough into the bottom of a spread bowl and even out. Starting in the center, using your knuckles, work your way around the bowl towards the outside. Dough will climb the sides of the bowl. Work the dough into a pie crust and when done, use your hands to smooth out. Put the bowl under a fan to dry for 6 to 8 hours. This crust needs to sit a little longer than others. While the crust dries, grab all your favorite ingredients to mix up for a filling.

One Sweet Chocolate Pie

Ingredients:
1 (16 oz) pkg Duplex cream cookies   hot water
1 cup hot chocolate mix   ¼ (18 oz) jar peanut butter
3 oatmeal cream pies
1 (3 oz) Ramen noodles (any flavor)
2 (1 oz) chick-o-sticks
1 (.81 oz) pkg French vanilla cappuccino

Directions: Separate cream from cookies and set cream aside. Set aside 16 vanilla halves from these cookies. This is equal to 8 (whole) cookies. Crush the rest of the cookies into a fine powder. Place all in a spread bowl, add 4 tbsps of water and knead into a pliable dough. Might need to add ½ tbsp of water, but no more as you knead. You do not want it too wet. Once kneaded, flatten into the bottom of the spread bowl and even out. Starting in the center and using your knuckles, press down firmly, working your way around the bowl towards the outside. Dough will climb the sides of the bowl. Use your hands and work it into a pie crust. Smooth out when done. Put the bowl under a fan to dry for 3 to 4 hours. While it dries, combine the 16 vanilla cookie halves, hot chocolate mix, peanut butter, and oatmeal cream pies. Now, using a full hot sauce bottle, crush up Ramen noodles into a fine powder. Better to crush 1/3 at a time in a noodles bag. Takes some time but make sure it is finely crushed. Add the powder to spread bowl with just shy of 1/3 a cup of water and knead well. Flatten this mixture into the bottom of the spread bowl and even out. Put this bowl under fan to dry with crust. Crush up the chick-o-sticks and put in an insert cup with the cappuccino and the cookie cream. Add ¼ tbsp hot water and stir. Place in a hot pot to melt until pie and filling are ready. When all is ready, take a spoon and run it around the hot chocolate mixture to loosen from sides. Turn bowl upside down and remove filling from bowl. Place it in the pie crust and press firmly. Remove insert from the hot pot and stir. Pour it over pie and even out. Place under a fan for another 1 ½ hours. Cut and serve. Sweeettt.

Butter-Chocolate Cream Pie

Ingredients: 1 (16 oz) pkg vanilla cream cookies   1 (12 oz) Sprite
1 cup hot chocolate mix   1 (43 grams) pkg oatmeal
2 (3.2 oz) pkgs instant milk
1 (.14 oz) lemon/orange sports drink mix
1 tbsp peanut butter   1 (1.74 oz) pkg peanut M&M's
1 (1 oz) chick-o-stick

Directions: Separate cream from cookies and set cream aside. Crush all cookies into a fine powder and put in a spread bowl. Add 5 ½ tbsps of Sprite to mixture and knead into a pliable dough. Do not make too wet. Once kneaded and starting in the center, press down firmly, working your way around the bowl towards the outside. Dough will climb the sides. Work the dough into a pie crust. Smooth out when done. Put bowl under a fan to dry for 2 to 3 hours. In a separate bowl, combine hot chocolate mix with 3 to 4 tbsps of hot water and mix well. Add one regular oatmeal to this mixture and knead. Flatten out the mixture into the bottom of a spread bowl and even out. Set this bowl with pie crust aside until crust is dry. When dry, use a spoon and run it around the bowl with the hot chocolate mix, turn bowl upside down, and remove filling from bowl. Place in the pie crust and press firmly all the way around. Rinse the bowl. Now, combine both instant milks, sports drink mix, and ¾ can (1 ¼ cups) of Sprite. Add Sprite very slowly as you whip. Better to use two spoons to whip. Should be smooth and creamy. No lumps. Once this is done, stir in peanut butter. Lightly crush M&M's and add to bowl. Stir until all is smooth. Pour this mixture into pie crust and smooth. Crush chick-o-stick and sprinkle on top. Put bowl under a fan for a full 8 hours. Cut into 8 slices and serve. Invite a couple of close friends. Must be eaten within 24 hours. You will crave for more! You can melt the cream from the cream cookies and drizzle on top or save it for another pie. This is really sweet enough.

Chocolate Almond Cherry Pie

Ingredients: 1 (16 oz) pkg vanilla cream cookies   ½ cup instant milk
                1 (.81 oz) French vanilla cappuccino
                2 Snickers candy bars   2 (4 oz) cherry pies

Directions: This pie will take a little bit of time, but it is worth the wait. Separate the cream from the cookies and set cream aside. Crush the cookies into a fine powder and put all in a spread bowl. Add 5 ½ tbsps of hot water and knead into a pliable dough. Once kneaded, flatten dough into the bottom of the bowl and even out. Going around bowl create 1" lip around pie. Put bowl under a fan to dry for 3 to 4 hours. While drying, combine the instant milk, cappuccino, and 4 tbsps of hot water in a small chip bag. Whip all. Now, cut up the Snickers bars into tiny pieces and add to bag. Place the bag in a hot pot to melt. Might need to add another tbsp of water but no more than that. Once pie is dry, remove bag from hot pot and pour mixture into pie and even out. Place the pie under a fan for 2 to 3 more hours. Now, separate pie filling from cherry pies and add to the cookie cream filling. Put this mixture in an insert cup, add 1 tbsp of water, and place in a hot pot to melt for 1 hour. Once melted and drying time is complete for the pie, pour icing over the pie and put back under fan for 2 to 3 more hours. The wait is over, cut and serve.

Chocolate Malt Ball Pie

Ingredients: 1 (16 oz) pkg Duplex cookies
                2 (3.2 oz) pkgs instant milk
                1 (.81 oz) pkg French vanilla cappuccino
                ¼ (16 oz) bottle chocolate syrup   1 (12 oz) Coca Cola
                1 pkg (14) malt balls

Directions: Separate cream from cookies and set cream aside. Crush all cookies as fine as possible and put in a spread bowl. Add 5 tbsps of water to bowl and knead into a pliable dough. Might need to add another ½ tbsp as you knead, but no more than that. Once kneaded, flatten dough into the bottom of the spread bowl and even out. Using your knuckles and starting in the center, press down firmly, working your way around the bowl towards the outside. Dough will climb the sides. Work this dough into a pie crust.

Use hands and smooth out when done. Put bowl under fan to dry for 3 to 4 hours. After the crust is dry, in a separate spread bowl, combine the instant milk, French vanilla cappuccino, chocolate syrup. Use 2 spoons and whip until smooth and creamy. While you are whipping, SLOWLY add ¾ can (1 ¼ cups) of Coke. Now, add 14 malt balls and stir. Pour this into the pie crust and put back under a fan for 8 hours. This is a chocolate lovers dream. Some units only sell malt balls during Christmas season. If you want to decorate, melt cream and drizzle over top of pie. If not, save cream for next pie or cake.

Snicker Doodle Delight

Ingredients: 1 ½ (16 oz) pkgs vanilla cream cookies
3 Snickers candy bars   3 tbsps hot chocolate mix
2 pkgs nutty bars   2 (3.2 oz) pkgs instant milk
2 (2 oz) pkgs salted peanuts

Directions: Separate cream from cookies and set cream aside. Crush all the cookies into a fine powder and put in a spread bowl. Add 6 ½ to 7 tbsps of water and knead into a pliable dough. Once kneaded, flatten dough in the bottom of the spread bowl and even out. Starting in the middle and using your knuckles, press down and work around the bowl all the way to the outside. Dough will work its way up the sides of the bowl. Work this into your pie crust. Once complete, use your hands to smooth the crust. Put the bowl under a fan for 3 to 4 hours to dry. While the crust is drying, cut the Snickers bars into pieces and put them in an insert cup to melt. While waiting, in a spread bowl combine hot chocolate mix, both packages of nutty bars, and instant milk. Add 7 tbsps of hot water and use 2 spoons to whip. You want it to be lump free. You might need to add another tbsp of water but wait until candy bars are melted to see. Once candy bars are melted, add them to mixture and whip again very well. It will be very thick. When crust is dry, pour mixture into crust and put back under the fan for 6 to 8 hours to dry. After 1 hour, rinse salt from peanuts and decorate the pie. This is worth the wait. Simply delicious!! You can save the cream from the cookies for a later time, or you can melt and drizzle on top of this pie. It is really sweet enough, but it will be a diabetic's dream. This is an 8 piece dream pie.

Reese's Pieces Pie

Ingredients: 1 (16 oz) pkg vanilla cream cookies
    1 cup hot chocolate mix   2 heaping tbsps peanut butter
    ¼ cup hot water
    1 (3 oz) Ramen noodles (any flavor)
    2 (1 oz) chick-o-sticks   1 brick graham crackers
    1 pkg sweetener
    2 (43 grams) pkgs maple brown sugar oatmeal

Directions: Separate cream from cookies and set cream aside. Crush the cookies as fine as possible and put in a spread bowl. Add 5 ½ tbsps of water to cookies and knead into a dough. Do not add too much water! Once kneaded, flatten into the bottom of the spread bowl. Starting in the center and using your knuckles, press down firmly all around bowl, working your way towards the outside. Dough will climb sides of bowl. Work this into your pie crust. Once formed, use your hands to smooth. Put this bowl under a fan to dry for 3 to 4 hours. While you wait, grab 2 more spread bowls. In 1 bowl combine 1 cup hot chocolate mix, 1tbsp peanut butter, and 2 tbsps hot water and mix well. Put the mixture in an insert cup and place in a hot pot to melt while pie crust dries.

Use a full hot sauce bottle to crush the Ramen noodles. Best to crush 1/3 at a time in the noodles bag. It takes work but make sure you crush to a fine powder. Now, crush the chick-o-sticks and the brick of graham crackers. In the second spread bowl, combine graham crackers, chick-o-sticks, 1 tbsp peanut butter, noodles mixture, sweetener, oatmeal, and 3 tbsps hot water. Knead all this very well. Can add another tbsp of hot water if necessary, but no more. Flatten this mixture in the bottom of the spread bowl and place it with pie crust until all is dry. Stir the cookie cream into the insert cup until all is melted. Put back in hot pot for 30 minutes. Take the bowl with the oatmeal mixture filling and turn it upside down, remove filling, and place it in the pie crust. Press down firmly. Pour mixture in insert cup over top and even all out. Put back under the fan 2 more hours. Cut and serve. This recipe takes a little time, but this pie is well worth the wait.

Raisin Nut Delight

Ingredients: 1 (16 oz) pkg vanilla cream/Duplex cookies

1 cup hot water	1 heaping tbsp instant coffee
2 heaping tbsps hot chocolate mix	
1 (3 oz) Ramen noodles (any flavor)	
2 (43 grams) pkgs raisin & spice oatmeal	
1 (43 grams) pkg regular oatmeal	
½ (2 oz) pkg salted peanuts	2 pkgs sweetener
3 oatmeal cream pies	1 (4 oz) serving raisins from tray
1 pkg nutty bars	20 pieces butterscotch candies

Directions: Separate cream from cookies and set cream aside. Put 14 cookie halves aside and crush the rest of the cookies as fine as possible and put in a spread bowl. Fill coffee cup with hot water, add the coffee and hot chocolate mix, and stir. Add 5 ½ tbsps of this mixture to bowl and knead into a pliable dough. Might need to add another ½ tbsp but no more than that. You do not want it too wet. Flatten dough into the bottom of a spread bowl and even out. Using your knuckles, press down in the center of the bowl, and work around bowl towards the outside. Dough will begin to climb sides. Use your hands and work dough into the pie crust. Smooth when done. Put this bowl under the fan for 3 to 4 hours.

While this is drying, crush Ramen noodles into a fine powder. Use a full hot sauce bottle to crush 1/3 of the noodles at a time in the noodle bag. Pour powder into a spread bowl. Spoon 6 tbsps coffee mixture into this and stir until all liquid is absorbed. Break 14 cookie pieces into quarters and add to bowl with both oatmeals, peanuts, sweeteners, cream pies, raisins, and nutty bars. (If you want, save a few of the peanuts and raisins to decorate) Knead all of this. Add 2 to 3 tbsps coffee mixture, just enough to get moist. Make sure this mixture is kneaded well. Now break up all the butterscotch candies and add all but 6 pieces to mixture. Knead candies into mixture. Flatten mixture into the bottom of the spread bowl and even out. Put this bowl under a fan with pie crust. When you have this done, put the cream from the cookies into an insert cup with just a tsp of hot water and stir. Place the cream in a hot pot to melt while crust dries. When crust is ready, remove oatmeal mixture from bowl by turning bowl upside down. Put the filling in the pie crust and press firmly. Remove cream from hot pot and pour over pie and smooth. Decorate pie with the candies and raisins and nuts, if you saved any. Put under fan for 1 ½ additional hours.

Cinnamon Twist Crunch

Ingredients: 1 (16 oz) pkg vanilla cream cookies   1 cup hot water
                 1 (3 oz) Ramen noodles (any flavor)
                 2 (43 grams) pkgs apple cinnamon oatmeal
                 1 (43 grams) pkg cinnamon & spice oatmeal
                 3 oatmeal cream pies   ½ (2 oz) pkg salted peanuts
                 1 cup hot chocolate mix   3 (.75 oz) pkgs cream cheese
                 5 butterscotch candies

You will need: 3 spread bowls

Directions: Separate cream from cookies. Set 14 cookie halves and
cream aside. Crush the rest of cookies as fine as possible and put all in the
first spread bowl. Add 3 ½ tbsps hot water and knead into a pliable dough.
Flatten dough into bottom of spread bowl. Start in center of bowl and work
dough into the pie crust. Smooth out when done. Set bowl under a fan to
dry for 2 hours. While waiting, crush Ramen noodles in the package 1/3 at a
time. Better to use a full hot sauce bottle to do it. Takes work but crush to a
powder. Put the powder in a second spread bowl. Add all the oatmeal
packages, oatmeal cream pies, peanuts, and 14 cookie halves. Better to
break them up a bit. Now, add 1/3 cup hot water to this bowl, knead and set
aside with crust. In the third bowl add the cup of hot chocolate mix with 3
tbsps hot water. Mix well and set aside until the crust is dry. Once crust is
dry, add cookie cream and the cream cheese to the insert cup and mix well.
Add 1 tbsp hot water and stir again. Sit this insert in a hot pot so all can
melt. By the time pie crust is ready, complete pie in this order. Remove hot
chocolate mixture from its bowl and put it inside pie crust. Work mixture so
it covers bottom of crust and a little of the sides. Now, take the oatmeal
mixture from its bowl and put on top of this. Press down all around so that it
creates the pie. Press down firmly. Remove insert cup from hot pot, stir,
and pour over pie. Smooth out. Quickly crush up butterscotch and decorate
pie. Sit back under fan for 2 ½ hours. Icing will set. Cut and serve.

Oatmeal Cream Pie

Ingredients: 1 (16 oz) pkg Duplex cream cookies
                 1 box (10 pkgs) instant oatmeal

10 (.75 oz) pkgs cream cheese   4 oatmeal cream pies
1 ½ tbsps peanut butter   1 pkg plain M&M's

Directions: Separate cream from the cookies and set cream aside. Crush all cookies as fine as possible. Put all in a spread bowl. Add 5 ½ tbsps hot water and knead into a pliable dough. Do not use too much water. Starting in the center of the bowl and using your knuckles, press firmly, working around bowl towards the outside. Dough will climb the sides of bowl. Work it into your pie crust. When finished, use your hands and smooth out. In a separate spread bowl, combine all oatmeal, cream cheese packages, oatmeal cream pies, peanut butter, and about 1/8 cup hot water. Knead all together well and flatten into the bottom of the spread bowl. Set aside until crust is dry. Once crust is dry, take bowl with oatmeal mixture and run a spoon around bowl to loosen mixture. Turn bowl upside down and work filling out. Place filling in the pie crust, press firmly, and even out. Put under fan for 1 hour. While you wait, put the cookie cream in an insert cup with ½ tbsp hot water and whip well. Place cookie cream in a hot pot to melt. After 1 hour, stir well, and pour over the top of the pie and smooth out. Decorate pie with the M&M's and put under a fan for 1 ½ hours longer. Cut and serve.

Oatmeal Apple Pie

Ingredients: 1 (16 oz) pkg Duplex cream cookies   ¼ cup hot water
1 (4 oz) apple pie
3 (43 grams) pkgs apple cinnamon & spice oatmeal
1 (2.75 oz) pkg apple cinnamon roll
1 (3 oz) Ramen noodles (any flavor)
1 pkg sweetener

Directions: Separate cream from the cookies and set cream and 14 cookie halves aside. Crush all the other cookies into a fine powder. Put all in a spread bowl and add 3 ½ tbsps hot water and knead into a pliable dough. Might need to add ½ tbsp water as you knead but no more. Do not make too wet. Once kneaded, flatten dough into the bottom of the spread bowl and even out. Starting in the center of the bowl, use your knuckles and press down firmly, working around bowl towards the outside. Dough will climb the sides of bowl. Work it into the pie crust. Once done, use your hands and smooth out. Put bowl under a fan for 2 to 3 hours to dry. While it is drying, separate filling from apple pie. Place the filling in an insert cup. Place crust in a separate spread bowl. Add packages of oatmeal to this bowl. Break up 14 cookie halves into quarters and cut up the cinnamon roll. Add all these ingredients to the bowl. Use a full hot sauce bottle to crush Ramen noodles into a fine powder. Best to crush 1/3 at a time in the noodles bag. Add noodles to bowl with 1/3 cup hot water and knead all well. Now, flatten into the bottom of the spread bowl and even out. Set it aside under a fan to dry while waiting on crust. Put the cookie cream in the insert cup with apple filling and 1 tbsp hot water. Stir well and place in a hot pot to melt. When crust is dry, run a spoon around the oatmeal mixture. Turn bowl upside down and remove mixture. Set down in a pie crust and press firmly. Add sweetener to insert cup and stir until melted. Pour the icing over pie and smooth. Put back under fan for 1½ hours. This pie will take you back to the free world.

Sweet Potato Pie

Ingredients: 1 (16 oz) pkg vanilla cream cookies
1 (3 oz) Ramen noodles (any flavor)
2 (43 grams) pkgs maple brown sugar oatmeal
1 (1 oz) chick-o-stick   1 (4 oz) serving raisins from tray
2 (4 oz) servings sweet potatoes from tray

Directions: Separate the cream from the cookies and set the cream and 14 cookie halves aside. Crush the rest of the cookies into a fine powder and put in a spread bowl. Add 3 ½ tbsps hot water and knead into a pliable dough. Do not make too wet, but might need to add ½ tbsp as you knead. Flatten mixture in the spread bowl and even out. Using your knuckles and starting in the center of the bowl, press down firmly, working your way around the bowl towards the outside. Dough will climb sides of bowl. Work the dough into the pie crust. Smooth out when done. Put the bowl under a fan for 2 to 3 hours to dry. Now, take a full hot sauce bottle and crush the Ramen noodles. Best to crush 1/3 at a time in the noodles bag. Take your time and make sure this is a powder. Get a separate spread bowl and combine the noodles with 1/3 cup hot water. Cover and let noodles absorb the water. Add the oatmeal, chick-o-stick, raisins, sweet potatoes and mix well. Break up and knead in the 14 cookie halves. Flatten in the spread bowl and even out. Put this bowl with the pie crust to dry. While waiting, put the cookie cream in an insert cup with a ½ tbsp water and mix well. Place it in a hot pot to melt until crust is dry. When all is ready, spoon sweet potato mixture into crust and even out. Pour icing over the top of pie. Spread evenly and put back under a fan for 1 ½ hours. Cut and serve. Best to eat this right away. Nice little treat.

End of the Road

Ingredients: 1 (16 oz) pkg cream cookies (any flavor)
                2 (1 oz) chick-o-sticks   20 pieces butterscotch candies
                1 (3 oz) Ramen noodles (any flavor)
                2 (43 grams) pkgs cinnamon & spice oatmeal
                1 heaping tbsp peanut butter   2 pkgs sweetener
                1 (4 oz) serving mixed fruit from tray

Directions: Separate cream from cookies and set cream and 14 cookie halves aside. Crush the rest of the cookies and place all in a spread bowl. Add 3 ½ tbsps hot water and knead into a pliable dough. Might need to add another ¼ to ½ tbsp of water as you knead, but no more than that. You do not want the dough too wet. Once kneaded, flatten dough into the bottom of the spread bowl and even out. Starting in the center of the bowl and using your knuckles, press down firmly, working your way around bowl. Use your hands and work this into your pie crust. Once done, use your hands and smooth out. Put this bowl under a fan to dry for 2 to 3 hours.

While you wait, crush chick-o-sticks and candies. Set a little candy aside to decorate pie. Get a full hot sauce bottle and crush the Ramen noodles into a fine powder. Best to crush just 1/3 at a time in the noodles bag. This takes a little work but make sure it is a fine powder. In a separate spread bowl, combine the oatmeal, crushed noodles, chick-o-sticks, peanut butter, candy, sweeteners, mixed fruit, and 1/3 cup hot water. Knead it well. Break the 14 cookies into quarters, add to bowl, and knead thoroughly. Flatten into the bottom of the spread bowl and even out. Put with pie crust to dry. While you wait, put the cookie cream into an insert cup with ½ tbsp hot water. Mix well and place in a hot pot to melt for 30 minutes. When crust is dry, run a spoon around the bowl with the oatmeal mixture in it. Turn bowl upside down and remove filling. Place in the pie crust and even out. Stir icing in insert cup and pour over pie and even out. Decorate pie with leftover candy and put back under fan for 1½ more hours. Cut and serve. You should inherit a friend or two with this one.

Double Fudge Deluxe

Ingredients:
1 (16 oz) pkg peanut butter cream cookies
½ bag (25 pieces) butterscotch candies
½ cup hot water   1 (3 oz) Ramen noodles (any flavor)
½ bag (2 lb) hot chocolate mix
3 (.75 oz) pkgs cream cheese
½ bag (2 oz) salted peanuts

Directions: Separate cream from cookies and set cream and 14 cookie halves aside. (You can substitute Duplex for peanut butter cream cookies) Start by making center of pie. Crush candy and put it in insert cup with 2 tbsps water. Put insert cup in a hot pot and fully melt candy. Crush Ramen noodles into a fine powder. It is better if you use a full hot sauce bottle and crush 1/3 at a time. It must be crushed to a fine powder. Combine the powder with melted candy, hot chocolate mix, and the 14 cookie halves in a spread bowl, and knead well. Flatten and even out in the bottom of the spread bowl. Put bowl under fan for 4 hours. While it is drying, crush the rest of the cookies into a fine powder and put in a separate spread bowl. Add 3 ½ tbsps of water and knead into a pliable dough. Might need to add another ½ tbsp of water as you knead, but no more than that. You do not want it too wet. Even out and smooth dough in the bottom of the spread bowl. Starting in the center of the bowl, using your knuckles, press down firmly, working your way around the bowl. Using your hands, work it into the pie crust and then smooth out. Place the bowl under a fan to dry for 2 to 3 hours. Once filling is ready, turn bowl upside down and remove. Set the filling into pie crust and press down firmly. Set aside to prepare icing. In the insert cup, combine cream filling with cream cheese. Add 1 tbsp water and stir well. Place insert cup in the hot pot for 30 minutes to melt. When done, whip and pour and smooth over pie. Rinse peanuts and decorate pie. Place under a fan for 2 more hours to set up. AWESOME!

Dream Bar Cake

Ingredients:
2 (16 oz) pkgs vanilla cream cookies
3 (.34 oz) pkgs orange sports drink mix
3 (.75 oz) pkgs cream cheese
1 (10.25 oz) bag orange slices

Directions: Separate cream from cookies and set cream aside. Crush all cookies as fine as possible. Divide cookies equally in 2 spread bowls. Put the sports drink mix in a coffee or insert cup, add ½ cup hot water and stir until all is dissolved. Fill cup the rest of the way with cold water and stir again. In each bowl add 5 ½ tbsps of the sports drink and knead into a pliable dough. If it is too dry, add another ½ tbsp of sports drink mix. Do not over do it. After all is kneaded well, turn bowls upside down and remove dough and set on plain white paper under a fan to dry for 2 hours. Depending on weather, might need a little more drying time. When dry, place the cookie cream, cream cheese, and 1 tbsp sports drink mix in an insert cup and place in a hot pot to heat for 30 minutes. Now, put one part of cake into a spread bowl. Cut up half the bag of orange slices and put on top of this cake. Top off with second piece of cake and press down firmly. Pour and smooth icing over cake. Decorate cake with the other half of the orange slices. Put the cake under a fan for 2 to 3 more hours. What a dream come true.

Peanut Butter & Jelly Cake

Ingredients: 2 (16 oz) pkgs vanilla/Duplex cream cookies
1 cup hot chocolate mix   2 heaping tbsps peanut butter
¼ (10 oz) bag sunflower seeds (optional)
¼ (12 oz) bottle grape jelly   2 (.75 oz) pkgs cream cheese

Directions: Separate cream from cookies and set cream aside. Crush all cookies as fine as possible and put in a large spread bowl. Add 9 ½ tbsps of water and knead into a pliable dough. You might need another ½ tbsp of water as you knead but no more. Separate dough into two even pieces and set one aside. Flatten one piece of dough into the bottom of the spread bowl and even out. Turn bowl upside down, remove dough and put under a fan to dry for 2 to 3 hours. Repeat this process with the other piece of dough. In a small bowl combine hot chocolate mix, cookie cream, and 2 tbsps of water and mix well. Pour the mixture into an insert cup and place in hot pot to heat while cake dries. Once cake is dry, put one piece back in bowl and layer with peanut butter and sunflower seeds. Mix jelly with cream cheese and place on top of the peanut butter and sunflower seeds. Place second piece of cake on top of this and press down a bit. Now pour hot chocolate mixture over the top and sprinkle with a few sunflower seeds. Put under a fan to dry for 2 to 3 more hours.

Mini Fruitcake

Ingredients: 8 chocolate chip/oatmeal cookies
2 (43 grams) pkgs apple cinnamon oatmeal
1 heaping tbsp peanut butter
1 heaping tbsp strawberry preserves
1 (2 oz) pkg trail mix

Directions: Crush the cookies and put in a spread bowl with the rest of the ingredients and not quite 1/3 cup of hot water. Knead together and form it into the shape you desire. Put it on plain white paper and place under a fan for 4 to 6 hours. Heat up the coffee, you will really enjoy this one.

Spice-E-Cake

Ingredients: 1 (16 oz) pkg vanilla cream cookies
3 fireball candies   2 (.75 oz) pkgs cream cheese
2 pkgs sweeteners

Directions: Separate cream from cookies and set cream aside. Crush cookies as fine as possible and put in a spread bowl. Add 5 ½ tbsps of water and knead into a pliable dough. Flatten dough in the bottom of the bowl and even out. Turn bowl upside down and remove cake. Place on plain white paper and put under a fan to dry for 3 to 4 hours. When dry, return cake to bowl. Crush the fireballs and put them in an insert cup. Add the cream cheese, sweeteners, and ½ tbsp hot water and dissolve. Add the cookie cream and whip. Place it in a hot pot to heat for 1 hour. Pour icing over cake and put under a fan for 2 more hours. Believe me, this is really a nice treat.

Convict Cake

Ingredients: 1 (16 oz) pkg vanilla cream cookies
¼ (16 oz) bottle chocolate syrup
3 tbsps butter (optional)
¼ (18 oz) jar peanut butter
2 cinnamon rolls (any size, any flavor)
¼ (12 oz) bottle strawberry preserves
1 pkg M&M's plain

Directions: Separate cream from cookies and set cream aside. Crush all cookies into a fine powder and put in a large spread bowl. Add 5 ½ tbsps hot water and knead into a pliable dough. Might need to add ½ tbsp as you knead but no more than that. Separate this dough into 2 even parts. In a spread bowl, mold one piece of dough to the bottom of the bowl and even out. Turn bowl upside down to remove and put on plain white paper to dry under a fan for 2 to 3 hours. Repeat this process with second piece. While drying, combine cookie cream, chocolate syrup, butter, and 1 tbsp of peanut butter in an insert cup and place in a hot pot to melt. Cut up the cinnamon rolls. When cake is dry, place one piece back in a spread bowl and cover with peanut butter, preserves, and cinnamon rolls. Place second piece on top and press down firmly. Remove icing from hot pot. Pour and smooth over top of cake. Decorate cake with M&M's. Put cake under a fan to dry for another 2 to 3 hours.

Baltimore's Magic Trick

Ingredients: 1 banana fudge ice cream bar
1 (16 oz) pkg cream cookies (any flavor)
¼ cup hot chocolate mix   1 (2 oz) pkg energy mix

Directions: Place the ice cream in a cup to melt as you prepare the rest. Separate cream from cookies and set cream aside. Crush cookies as fine as possible and put all in a spread bowl. Add the hot chocolate mix to bowl with 7 ½ tbsps of hot water and knead into a pliable dough. Once kneaded, flatten dough into the bottom of the spread bowl and even out. Go around bowl and make a lip about ¾ inch. Place this bowl under a fan to dry for 1 to 2 hours. While cake is drying, put the cookie cream into an insert cup with ½ tbsp water and place in a hot pot to melt. When cake is dry, add the ice cream to the cream and whip really well. Spread the energy mix inside the lip of cake. Pour icing over the top of cake and put under the fan for 3 to 4 more hours. Now comes the magic trick: Cut cake and watch it disappear!!

Simply a Chocolate Cake

Ingredients: 1 (16 oz) pkg vanilla cream cookies
1 cup hot chocolate mix   1 plain Hershey bar

Directions: Separate cream from cookies and set cream aside. Crush all cookies into a fine powder and put in a spread bowl with the hot chocolate mix. Add 5 ½ tbsps of hot water to bowl and knead into a pliable dough. Once kneaded, flatten into the bottom of the bowl and even out. Run a spoon around dough to loosen from the sides of bowl. Put this bowl under a fan for 4 hours to dry. While drying, put cookie cream in an insert cup with 1 tbsp hot water. Stir well and place in a hot pot to melt. When cake is dry, pour icing over the top. Quickly take a razor blade and shave the Hershey bar all over the top of the cake to decorate. Put under a fan for another 2 hours. This will make 8 people happy, once cut.

Sweet Snickers Cake

Ingredients: 4 Snicker's candy bars   4 (.75 oz) pkgs cream cheese
1 (16 oz) pkg vanilla cream cookies

Directions: Cut the Snickers bars into small pieces. Put all pieces and the cream cheese in an insert cup and place in a hot pot to melt fully. While it is melting, separate cream from cookies and add the cream to the insert cup. Might need to add 1 tbsp hot water as well. Stir well. Now, crush all cookies as fine as possible and put in a spread bowl. Add 5 tbsps hot water and knead into a pliable dough. Once kneaded, flatten into the bottom of the spread bowl and even out. Put this bowl under a fan to dry for 3 hours. Can run a spoon around bowl to loosen from the sides. When dry, remove icing from hot pot, whip well, and pour and smooth over the top of cake. Put this under a fan for another 2 hours. You are gonna love this one. MMM, MMM, good!

Chocolate-Toffee Cake

Ingredients: 1 (16 oz) pkg Duplex cream cookies
½ bag (25 pcs) butterscotch candies
1 (.81 oz) pkg French vanilla cappuccino
1 cup hot chocolate mix

Directions: Separate cream from cookies and set cream aside. Crush all cookies into a fine powder and put in a spread bowl. Add 5 tbsps hot water and knead into a pliable dough. Do not make it too wet. Flatten the dough in the bottom of the spread bowl and even out. Put the bowl under a fan to dry for 3 hours. To help dry a little, run a spoon around bowl to loosen the dough from the sides. While it is drying, crush all candies. In an insert cup, combine candies, cappuccino, and cookie cream. Add 2 tbsps hot water to cup and place in a hot pot to melt fully. Once melted, add the hot chocolate mix to insert cup, stir well, and leave in hot pot to heat until cake is fully dry. Once cake is dry, pour icing and smooth over the top. Put under a fan for 2 hours. This one is simply great!

Gravitational Bliss

Ingredients: 2 (16 oz) pkgs Duplex cookies
                2 heaping tbsps peanut butter   2 Snickers bars
                4 (.78 oz) Rice Crispy treats   8 oatmeal cream pies
                ½ cup hot chocolate mix   2 (1 oz) chick-o-sticks
                4 pkgs nutty bars
                1 (8 oz) pkg Bud's best Butterfinger cookies
                1 pkg M&M's plain

Directions: Separate cream from cookies and set cream aside. Crush all
cookies as fine as possible and put in a spread bowl. Add 8 ½ tbsps hot
water and knead into a pliable dough. Might need to add ½ to 1 tbsp more
water as you knead, but do not make too wet. Once kneaded, separate
mixture into 2 equal parts. Flatten one part in the spread bowl, remove from
bowl, and place on plain white paper under a fan to dry for 2 to 3 hours.
Repeat with the second piece. While they dry, place the cookie cream, 1 tbsp
hot water, and 1 ½ tbsps peanut butter in an insert cup. Stir well and place in
the hot pot to melt for 1 ½ hours. Stir occasionally. Cut up the Snickers
bars and Rice Crispy treats. Use your ID and separate all the oatmeal cream
pies in half. In a separate spread bowl, combine hot chocolate mix, the rest
of the peanut butter, and 3 tbsps hot water. Whip until smooth and creamy.
Once dough has dried, place one piece back in a spread bowl and layer cake
in this order: a layer of peanut butter mixture, half the chick-o-sticks, half
the Snickers bars, 2 packages nutty bars, half the Rice Crispy treats, and 1/3
of the Bud's best cookies. Take half of the 16 oatmeal cream pies and cap
this off. Press down firmly. Repeat all these steps. Now, take the rest of the
Bud's best cookies and spread over the cake. Remove insert cup from hot
pot, stir well, and pour over cake. Even it out. Decorate with M&M's. Place
under a fan to dry for 3 to 4 hours. This is one special treat for you and a
couple close associates.

Chocolate Coconut Cake

Ingredients: 1 (16 oz) pkg vanilla cream cookies
                1 (16 oz) pkg vanilla wafers   10 (1 oz) chick-o-sticks
                1 cup hot chocolate mix

Directions: Separate cream from cookies and set cream aside. Crush all cookies, vanilla wafers, and chick-o-sticks as fine as possible and mix together in a spread bowl. Add 10 tbsps hot water and knead into a pliable dough. You do not want it too wet but might need to add another ½ tbsp as you knead. Flatten dough into the bottom of the bowl and even out. Put the bowl under a fan for 3 to 4 hours to dry. While drying, combine the hot chocolate mix, cookie cream, and 2 tbsps of hot water in an insert cup and mix well. Put the cup in a hot pot to melt. When cake is dry, pour and smooth icing over the top. Put it under a fan to dry for another 2 hours.

Sweet Strawberry Cake

Ingredients: 1 (16 oz) pkg vanilla cream cookies
1 (16 oz) pkg vanilla wafers
4 (43 grams) pkgs strawberry instant oatmeal
1 (12 oz) strawberry soda
2 tbsps strawberry preserves

Directions: Separate cream from cookies and set cream aside. Crush all vanilla wafers and cookies as fine as possible and combine in a spread bowl. Add the oatmeal and 10 tbsps of soda and knead thoroughly. You might need another ½ to 1 tbsp of soda as you knead but must be really careful. You do not want it too wet. Once kneaded, flatten dough into the bottom of the spread bowl and even out. Put the bowl under a fan to dry for 3 to 4 hours. While drying, put the cookie cream in an insert cup with the strawberry preserves. Place in a hot pot to melt at least 1 hour and stir occasionally. When cake is dry, remove insert cup from hot pot and pour over the top of cake. Smooth and put under a fan for 2 more hours. Simply the best.

The Real Deal Cake

Ingredients: 1 (16 oz) box oatmeal cream pies
2 (3 oz) Ramen noodles (any flavor)
1 (12 oz) Sprite   4 pkgs sweeteners
1 (16 oz) pkg vanilla cream cookies

You will need:
2 (1 oz) chick-o-sticks	2 pkgs nutty bars
1 empty toilet paper roll	1 small trash bag

Directions: Cut a trash bag to cover the toilet paper roll. Cut a second piece that will cover the inside of the spread bowl as well as overlap about 2 inches. Set the rest of the bag aside. Split 8 oatmeal cream pies in half using your ID card. Place the toilet paper roll on the center of the spread bowl, standing up. Now, cream side facing down, layer your bowl to form a pie crust. You do not want any gaps. Better to start in the center and work your way out. Set this bowl aside.

Grab a full hot sauce bottle and crush the noodles. Better to crush 1/3 of each package at a time. It will take time and effort but make sure it is powder when done. Put the powder in a separate spread bowl and pour in the Sprite and 1/3 can (a little more than ½ cup) of hot water. Stir and cover for 10 minutes. Then, stir in the sweeteners. Separate the cream from the cookies and set cream aside. Crush chick-o-sticks and nutty bars. Get the bowl with the crust in it and layer bowl in this order: 1 row of cookies, spread evenly, thin layer noodle mixture, 1 chick-o-stick, and one nutty bar. Repeat this layering. Top with last row of cookies and last layer of Ramen mixture. Take last 4 oatmeal cream pies, split in half and with cream side down, cover top of bowl. Some gaps are okay. Press down <u>FIRMLY</u>. Cover this with the plastic bag and put in a safe place for 24 hours.

After 24 hour period, flip bowl over and remove bowl. Press down firmly one more time before you remove plastic. Place the cookie cream in an insert cup with ½ tbsp hot water and whip. Place insert in a hot pot to melt for 30 minutes. Stir well and pour all the icing, evenly, around cake. Allow to run down. Let dry 2 hours. Cut and serve. This is one of the best cakes you will ever eat! That's why it is called, The Real Deal!!!!

Texas Mudd

Ingredients:
1 (12 oz) pkg chocolate chip cookies	
½ (8 oz) bag chocolate covered peanuts	
1 Snickers bar	1 (1 oz) chick-o-stick
4 malt balls	1 Hershey bar plain
1 (2 oz) chocolate moon pie	

Directions: Crush cookies into a fine powder. Add 3 ½ tbsps hot water and knead into a pliable dough. Might need another ½ tbsp of water but be very careful not to make too wet. Once kneaded, separate into 2 equal parts. Divide the chocolate covered peanuts between the two pieces and knead. Flatten one piece into the bottom of a spread bowl and even out. Turn bowl upside down and remove. Put it on plain, white paper to dry. Repeat with second piece. They will dry in about 3 hours. While waiting, cut up the Snickers bar and crush the chick-o-stick. Smash malt balls and break up Hershey bar. Combine all these ingredients in an insert cup and place in a hot pot to melt. Might need to add ½ tbsp hot water to help melt. Now, separate the cookie part from marshmallow part of the moon pie. When dry, place one part of the dough back into the spread bowl. Remove insert from hot pot and stir well. Pour a layer of mixture on cookie dough, cut up marshmallow into pieces, and top mixture. Now, place second piece of dough on top of this layer, and pour on the rest of the chocolate mixture. Make even and put under a fan for 2 to 3 hours. Wow, what a delight!!

Big Red Apple Cheesecake

Ingredients:
- 1 (13 oz) box honey graham crackers
- 2 (3.2 oz) pkgs instant milk
- 1 (.34 oz) pkg lemon lime sports drink/cooloff
- 1 (12 oz) Big Red soda   5 (.75 oz) pkgs cream cheese
- 3 (43 grams) pkgs apple cinnamon oatmeal

Directions: Crush the graham crackers and put all in a spread bowl. Add 5 tbsps of water and knead into a pliable dough. Might need to add another ½ tbsp as you knead. Be careful not to overdo it with water. Flatten dough in the bottom of the spread bowl and even out. Using your knuckles and starting in the center of dough, push down and work around bowl to work dough up the sides of the bowl. You now have the pie crust. Once crust is formed, use your hands to smooth the crust. Put the bowl under a fan to dry for 3 to 4 hours. When dry, in a separate spread bowl combine instant milk and sports drink/cooloff and slowly pour in ¾ can (1 ¼ cups) Big Red as you whip. Two spoons work best for whipping. You want it smooth and creamy. No lumps! Once this is done, add the cream cheese and whip again. Stir in the instant oatmeal. Pour this mixture into the pie crust and put under a fan for 6 to 8 hours to dry. If still wet, then leave till dry.

Cheesecake #1

Ingredients:
- 1 (13 oz) box honey graham crackers
- 2 (3.2 oz) pkgs instant milk
- 1 (.34 oz) pkg lemon lime sports drink/cooloff
- 1 (12 oz) Sprite   5 (.75 oz) pkgs cream cheese

Directions: Crush all graham crackers and put in a spread bowl. Add 5 tbsps water and knead into a pliable dough. If too dry, add ½ tbsp at a time until you have a pliable dough. Flatten dough in the bottom of a spread bowl and even out. Using your knuckles, press down starting in the center of the bowl, working around bowl towards the outside. Dough will climb the sides of the bowl. Work it into a pie crust. Once crust is formed, smooth out. Put the crust under a fan to dry for 3 to 4 hours. When crust is dry, get another spread bowl and combine the instant milk with the sports drink/cooloff. As you whip the mixture, slowly pour ¾ of the Sprite (about 1 ¼ cups) in until it is smooth and creamy. You want no lumps. Using two spoons works best for this. Drink the rest of the Sprite. Add all the cream cheese packages to bowl. Whip until smooth and creamy. Pour this into pie crust and level out. Put under a fan for 8 hours. Cut and serve yourself and a couple friends. You want to eat this within 24 hours.

Cheesecake #2

Ingredients: 1 (16 oz) pkg vanilla cream cookies
                          15 (.75 oz) pkgs cream cheese
                          4 pkgs sweeteners   1 brick graham crackers

Directions: Separate cream from cookies and set cream aside. Crush all cookies as fine as possible and put in a spread bowl. Add 5 ½ tbsps water to mix and knead into a pliable dough. Flatten dough into the bottom of a spread bowl and even out. Using your knuckles, work from the center out and press down as you work the dough up the sides of the bowl. Once pie crust is formed, use your hands to smooth out. Put the pie crust under a fan to dry for 3 to 4 hours. When pie crust is dry, combine the cookie cream, the cream cheese packages, and the sweeteners in a small spread bowl. Mix all well. Can even melt a bit. Make sure it is smooth and creamy. Pour mixture into crust and even out. Crush up the brick of graham crackers and sprinkle on top. Put it under a fan for 8 hours. Cut and serve with your favorite drink.

Strawberry Cheesecake

Ingredients:
   1 (16 oz) pkg vanilla/Duplex cream cookies*
   1 (12 oz) Sprite
   2 (3.2 oz) pkgs instant milk
   1 (.34 oz) pkg lemon lime sports drink/cooloff
   5 (.75 oz) pkgs cream cheese
   ¼ (12 oz) bottle strawberry preserves
   *Graham crackers can substitute for cream cookies

Directions: Separate cream from cookies and set cream aside. Crush cookies into a fine powder and put in spread bowl. Add 5 ½ tbsps of Sprite and knead into a pliable dough. Do not use too much Sprite. If you use graham crackers, start with 5 tbsps of Sprite. Flatten dough into the bottom of the spread bowl and even out. Using your knuckles and starting in the center of the dough, press down as you work around the bowl. Work the dough up the sides of the bowl to form the crust. Once crust is formed, smooth with your hands. Put bowl under a fan to dry 3 to 4 hours. When ready, use a separate spread bowl and combine the instant milk, sports drink/cooloff, and slowly add ¾ can of Sprite (1 ¼ cups) as you whip. Using two spoons works best for whipping. You want the mixture smooth and creamy. No lumps! When done, add the cream cheese and whip again. Pour mixture into the pie crust. Put bowl under a fan for 6 to 8 hours. When you are ready to cut pie, pour on strawberry preserves and spread evenly. This is a really tasty treat.

Strawberry Cheesecake #2

Ingredients:
   1 (16 oz) pkg Duplex cookies 1 (12 oz) strawberry soda
   1 pint strawberry ice cream 1 (3.2 oz) pkg instant milk
   4 (.75 oz) pkgs cream cheese 1 Snickers candy bar

Directions: Separate cream from cookies and set cream aside. Crush Duplex cookies as fine as possible and put all in a spread bowl. Add 5 tbsps of the strawberry soda and knead into a pliable dough. Flatten dough into the bottom of the spread bowl and even out. Using your knuckles and starting in the center of the dough, press down firmly, and work your way around the bowl towards the outside. Dough will climb the sides of the bowl. Work this into your pie crust. Once done, smooth out with your hands. Put the bowl under a fan to dry for 2 to 3 hours. By the time the crust is dry, the ice cream should be melted. In a separate spread bowl, combine the ice cream, instant milk, and cream cheese and whip. As you whip, slowly pour in ¾ can of the strawberry soda (1 ¼ cups). Using two spoons works best. Whip until smooth and creamy. You want no lumps. Pour into crust and even out. Put it under a fan to dry for 8 hours. About 2 hours before time is up, combine cream from cookies with candy bar in an insert cup and melt in hot pot. Pour the melted bar over the pie and smooth out. After 2 hours, it is time to cut and serve. You will talk about this one for days. Truly a masterpiece.

Root Beer Float Pie

Ingredients: 1 (13 oz) box graham crackers   1 (12 oz) root beer soda
2 (3.2 oz) pkgs instant milk
1 (.34 oz) pkg lemon lime sports drink/cooloff

Directions: Crush all graham crackers into a fine powder and place into a spread bowl. Spoon in 5 tbsps of root beer and knead thoroughly. Add ½ tbsp of root beer if needed. Do not make too wet. Once kneaded, flatten dough evenly in the bottom of a spread bowl. Using your knuckles and starting in the center, press down and work dough up the sides of the bowl. Once formed, use your hands to smooth the dough. Put pie crust under a fan to dry for 3 to 4 hours. When crust is dry, in a separate spread bowl, combine instant milk and lemon lime sports drink/cooloff and slowly pour in the root beer as you whip. Using two spoons works best. Whip the mixture until all is smooth and creamy. Pour mixture into pie crust and level out. Place under a fan to dry for 6 to 8 hours. If not dry all the way, let sit a little longer. Cut and serve.

Cupcake Cheesecake

Ingredients: 1 (13 oz) box graham crackers   1 (12 oz) Sprite
1 cup hot chocolate mix   2 (3.2 oz) pkgs instant milk
1 (.34 oz) pkg lemon lime sports drink
5 (.75 oz) pkgs cream cheese
2 pkgs chocolate cream cupcakes

Directions: Crush all graham crackers into a fine powder and put in a spread bowl. Add 5 ½ tbsps of Sprite and knead into a pliable dough. Do not make too wet. Once kneaded, use your knuckles and starting in the center of the bowl, press down firmly while you work your way all around bowl towards the outside. Dough will climb the sides of the bowl. Use your hands and work the mixture into a pie crust. Smooth when done. Put this bowl under a fan for 3 hours.

In a separate spread bowl, add 3 ½ tbsps hot water to hot chocolate mix and stir well. Do not over-water. You just want it moist. Put the mixture in an insert cup and place in a hot pot for 1 ½ hours. After it cooks, put back into a spread bowl, flatten out, and set aside while crust dries. Once crust is dry, turn bowl with hot chocolate mix upside down and remove the mixture. Place the mixture inside pie crust and press firmly all around. Set aside. Combine the instant milk, the sports drink mix, and slowly add ¾ can of Sprite (1 ¼ cups) as you whip until smooth and creamy. Best to use two spoons to whip. No lumps. Once ready, add the cream cheese to mixture and whip again. Once smooth and creamy, open packages of cupcakes, put each inside pie crust, then pour milk mixture into crust, around cupcakes. Put this bowl under a fan and dry for 8 hours. Cut and serve. This is one incredible dish.

Ice cream Cheesecake

Ingredients: 1 (16 oz) pkg cream cookies (any flavor)
1 (12 oz) Sprite   2 (3.2 oz) pkgs instant milk
1 (.43 grams) pkg maple brown sugar oatmeal
1 (.34 oz) pkg lemon lime sports drink/cooloff
1 pint favorite ice cream   5 (.75 oz) pkgs cream cheese
1 (2 oz) pkg salted peanuts

Directions: Separate cream from cookies and set cream aside. Crush cookies as fine as possible and put in a spread bowl. Put 5 ½ tbsps of Sprite in crushed cookies and knead into a pliable dough. Might need to add ¼ tbsp hot water. Be very careful not to make too wet. Smash dough to the bottom of the spread bowl and even out. Starting in the center and using knuckles, work dough out and up the sides of the bowl. Take your time to form the pie crust. Use your hands and smooth crust. Put crust under a fan to dry for 3 to

4 hours. Ice cream should be melted by now. In a separate spread bowl combine instant milk, oatmeal, and lemon lime sports drink/cooloff. Slowly add ice cream as you stir. Once this is done, slowly pour in ½ can (3/4 cup) of Sprite as you whip. Two spoons is best for this. Whip until smooth and creamy. Once complete, stir in all cream cheese packages and whip again until no lumps. Melt cream filling in hot pot and stir into mixture. Once all this is complete, pour mixture into pie crust and put back under a fan to dry for 2 hours. Rinse peanuts and add to the top of pie. Put under fan for another 8 hours. Now cut and serve. Should eat within 24 hours.

Banana Nut Cheesecake

Ingredients:
1 pint banana nut ice cream
1 (16 oz) box oatmeal cream pies
2 (2 oz) pkgs energy mix   2 (3.2 oz) pkgs instant milk
2 tbsps chocolate syrup   2 pkgs chocolate cup cakes

Directions: Set the ice cream aside to melt. Using your ID card, separate the oatmeal cream pies. Carefully cover the bottom and sides of a spread bowl with the oatmeal cream pies, cream side facing up. Form a pie crust and leave no gaps. Open packages of energy mix, remove the banana chips and set aside. In a separate spread bowl combine the ice cream, instant milk, chocolate syrup, and energy mix. Use two spoons and whip until all is smooth and creamy. Take your time and leave no lumps. Take the 4 cupcakes and put in the center of the pie crust. Pour the ice cream mixture into crust, over and around cupcakes. Hydrate the banana chips in a little hot water. Decorate the cake with them. Put cheesecake under a fan to dry for 4 to 6 hours.

Cappuccino Crunch Cheesecake

Ingredients:
1 (16 oz) pkg vanilla cream cookies   1 (12 oz) Sprite
2 (3.2 oz) pkgs instant milk
2 (.81 oz) pkgs French vanilla cappuccino   ½ cup sugar
1 (.34 oz) pkg lemon lime sports drink
5 (.75 oz) pkgs cream cheese   3 (1 oz) chick-o-sticks

Directions: Separate cream from cookies and set cream aside. Crush all cookies into a fine powder and place in a spread bowl. Add 5 tbsps of Sprite and knead into a pliable dough. Might need to add ½ tbsp as you knead. Using your knuckles and starting in the center of the bowl, press down firmly, working your way around the bowl towards the outside. Dough will climb the sides. Work it into a pie crust and smooth out once done. Put bowl under a fan for 2 to 3 hours to dry. When crust is dry, combine instant milk, cappuccino, sugar, and sports drink mix in another spread bowl. Slowly add ¾ can Sprite (1 ¼ cups) to bowl as you whip. Take your time, you want it smooth and creamy. Add the cream cheese and whip again. Crush all chick-o-sticks and stir into this mixture. Pour mixture into pie crust and put back under a fan for 8 hours. Cut into 8 slices and serve. Do not be afraid to try other flavors of cappuccino. You can top off with cream from cookies but it is not necessary. Use cream for another creation.

Maple Syrup Cheesecake

Ingredients: 1 (16 oz) pkg vanilla cream cookies   1 (12 oz) Sprite
                2 (3.2 oz) pkgs instant milk
                1 (.34 oz) pkg lemon lime sports drink mix
                ½ cup pancake syrup (save a bit for drizzling over cake)

Directions: Separate cream from cookies and set cream aside. Crush all cookies as fine as possible and place in a spread bowl. Add 5 ½ tbsps Sprite to bowl and knead into a pliable dough. Do not make too wet. Flatten dough into the bottom of the spread bowl and even out. Using your knuckles and starting in the center, press down firmly, working your way around bowl toward the outside. Dough will climb the sides. Work this mixture into a pie crust. Use your hands to smooth out. Put the bowl under a fan to dry for 3 to 4 hours. Once dry, in a separate spread bowl, combine instant milk, cream from cookies, sports drink mix, syrup, and ¾ can of Sprite (1 ¼ cups) and whip. You want it smooth and creamy. No lumps. Pour the mixture into the pie crust and put under fan for 8 hours to dry. Once dry, you can drizzle a little syrup over cheese cake for decoration. Most cheesecakes require cream cheese, this one does not.

Dr Pepper Cheesecake

Ingredients: 1 (13 oz) box graham crackers
2 (3.2 oz) pkgs instant milk
1 (.34 oz) pkg lemon lime sports drink mix
1 (12 oz) Dr Pepper
5 (.75 oz) pkgs cream cheese   1 (1 oz) chick-o-stick

Directions: Crush all the graham crackers and place in a spread bowl. Make sure they are crushed to a fine powder. Add 5 ½ to 6 tbsps of water and knead into a pliable dough. Do not use too much water. Using your knuckles and starting in the center, press down firmly and work your way around bowl towards the outside. Dough will climb sides of bowl. Work dough into a pie crust and smooth out when done. Put bowl under fan to dry for 3 to 4 hours. When crust is dry, combine the instant milk and the lemon lime sports drink mix. Begin whipping and slowly add ¾ can of Dr Pepper (1 ¼ cups) while you whip. Two spoons for the whipping is best. Whip until all is smooth and cream. No lumps. Now, add all cream cheese and whip again until smooth. Pour mixture into pie crust and level out. Put under a fan for 1 hour. Smash chick-o-stick and sprinkle over the top. Put under a fan to dry for 8 hours. Cut into 8 pieces and invite a few close friends. Must eat within 24 hours.

One Sweet Treat

Ingredients: 2 (16 oz) pkgs vanilla cream cookies
1 (12 oz) Coca-Cola   1 (2 lbs) bag hot chocolate mix
½ (18 oz) jar peanut butter   3 tbsps butter
50 (1 oz) chick-o-sticks

You will need: small trash bag

Directions: Separate cream from cookies and set cream aside. Crush cookies as fine as possible. Use two separate spread bowls and in each, combine half the Coca-Cola, half the cookies, half the hot chocolate mix, and half the peanut butter. Knead the ingredients in each bowl thoroughly. Do not be afraid to get your hands dirty. When finished, cut open trash bag and lay on bunk. Take the butter and coat the bag to avoid sticking. Empty one bowl of the mixture onto the bag. Coat a full soda can with butter to use as a roller. Roll out mixture on bag. Roll it out pretty thin. Now, open all chick-o-sticks. One by one lay a chick-o-stick on mixture and wrap the mixture around the chick-o-stick. Repeat with second bowl. Give or take, you should use all mixture and chick-o-sticks. After all are wrapped, place cookie cream in an insert cup and place in a hot pot to melt. Add ¾ tbsp of hot water. Once melted, drizzle icing over the top of the treats. Put all under a fan to dry for 3 hours. You will make lots of friends with these!!

Sweet Treat 2

Ingredients: ½ (13 oz) box graham crackers
1 cup hot chocolate mix   1 heaping tbsp peanut butter
1 box (10 pkgs) instant oatmeal

12 (1 oz) mint sticks/fruit sticks
You will need: small trash bag

Directions: Crush the graham crackers as fine as possible and set aside. In a large spread bowl combine hot chocolate mix, peanut butter, oatmeal, and about 1/3 cup of hot water. Mix and knead well. Get your hands in there to knead. Cut open the trash bag and lay it on your bunk. If possible, get some butter to coat bag and the soda can that you will use as a roller. Pour oatmeal mixture onto bag and use a full soda can to roll out mixture fairly thin. Now, open all the mint/fruit sticks. One by one lay mint/fruit sticks onto oatmeal mixture and roll the oatmeal mixture around mint/fruit sticks. Once all are coated, pour the graham crackers onto a clean chip bag and roll the treats in graham crackers. When finished, put the treats under a fan to dry for 3 to 4 hours.

Caramel Clusters

Ingredients: 4 (2 oz) pkgs peanuts
2 (8 oz) bags Bud's Best Butterfinger cookies
20 (1 oz) chick-o-sticks
6 Milky Way candy bars

Directions: Rinse salt from peanuts. Crush cookies and chick-o-sticks. In a large spread bowl combine these items and mix. Cut up all the candy bars and put pieces in an insert cup. Place insert in a hot pot and melt fully. Pour melted mixture into cookie mixture and stir together. Takes a little work. Once done, place a plastic bag or a clean chip bag on your bunk. Use a spoon to divide mixture. Drop mixture on bag and press down lightly. No certain shape. Should make about 50 pieces. Dry under a fan for 4 hours. What an awesome treat.

Coffee Delights

Ingredients: 1 (16 oz) pkg cream cookies (any flavor)
1 pkg nutty bars   1 oatmeal cream pie
1 cup hot coffee   5 tbsps hot chocolate mix
3 tbsps peanut butter

Directions: Separate cream from cookies and set cream aside. Crush cookies as fine as possible. Crush nutty bar and oatmeal cream pie and combine all in a spread bowl. Add 5 ½ tbsps of hot coffee to the mixture and knead into a pliable dough. Divide dough into equal parts and roll into balls. You want them about the size of half dollars. Place the balls on plain white paper and using your thumb, make an indentation in each one. Now, in a small bowl combine the cookie cream, hot chocolate mix, peanut butter, and 2 ½ tbsps hot coffee. Whip this mixture until smooth and creamy. You want it thick like icing. Pour ½ tbsp of icing into indentations of each ball and put back on paper. Put them under a fan to dry for 4 to 6 hours. Very tasty treat!!

Strawberry Dream Treats

Ingredients:
1 (16 oz) pkg strawberry cream cookies
2 (43 grams) pkgs strawberry instant oatmeal
1 (12 oz) strawberry soda
3 (.75 oz) pkgs cream cheese
1 tsp strawberry Kool-Aid

Directions: Separate cream from cookies and set cream aside for another recipe. Crush cookies as fine as possible and put in a spread bowl. Add instant oatmeal to bowl and mix. Add 6 tbsps strawberry soda and knead into a pliable dough. Place this mixture into a clean chip bag and flatten evenly. Cut open bag and put under a fan to dry for 3 to 4 hours. When dry, spread cream cheese over mixture evenly. Use Kool-Aid as decoration. Do not need too much, just add a little taste.

Baltimore's Butterscotch Brownies

Ingredients:
1 (16 oz) pkg vanilla wafers
1 (7.5 oz) pkg butterscotch candies
2 cups hot chocolate mix   hot water

Directions: You can substitute double fudge cookies for the vanilla wafers. If you use the double fudge cookies, separate the cream from the cookies and set the cream aside. To begin, crush cookies/wafers and put in a spread bowl. Crush all the candy into fairly small pieces. Divide candy into two equal parts. Put half the candy in spread bowl with cookies and add the hot chocolate mix. Once combined, slowly add a few tbsps of hot water and knead into a thick, pliable dough. This should only be moist, not wet. Place the mixture into a clean chip bag and flatten like a pizza. Cut open bag and put it under a fan to dry for 3 to 4 hours. While it begins to dry, put other half of the candy in a coffee cup with just a tbsp or two of hot water. Stir until all the candy is melted. If it does not melt completely, put it in an insert cup and place in hot pot. Once all is melted, add 2 tbsps hot chocolate mix and whip. If you have peanut butter, add ½ tbsp as well. Once whipped, pour over brownie and spread evenly. After all is dry, cut, eat and be happy! If you used the double fudge cookies, the cream will be added to icing for topping.

Armadillo Eggs

Ingredients: 7 chocolate chip cookies   5 vanilla wafers
1 pkg plain M&M's   ½ cup hot chocolate mix
hot water

Directions: Crush the chocolate chip cookies and the vanilla wafers. Keep them separated. Lightly crush the M&M's. In a spread bowl combine the chocolate chip cookies, hot chocolate mix, and the M&M's. Add about 4 tbsps of hot water and knead into a dough mixture. Should be moist but not wet. Divide mixture into several equal parts. Roll all into balls about the size of a quarter. Now, roll the balls in the vanilla wafers to coat. Place all on plain white paper under a fan to dry for 2 to 3 hours.

Chocolate Munchkins

Ingredients: 1 (16 oz) pkg Duplex cream cookies
2 heaping tbsps peanut butter
1 heaping tbsp plantation blend coffee

Directions: Separate cream from cookies and set cream aside. Crush cookies as fine as possible. In a spread bowl combine cookies and peanut butter. In a coffee cup, mix the coffee with 2 tbsps hot water and stir until dissolved. Pour it into cookie mixture and knead into a dough type substance. Might need to add another tbsp of hot water. Do not want too wet. Divide the mixture into equal parts and roll into balls. Do not make too large. Put them on plain white paper and dry under a fan for 1 hour. While they dry, put cookie cream in a hot pot insert and place in a hot pot to melt. Pour cream over munchkins and dry another 2 hours or so. Delicious!!!

Cream filled Chocolate

Ingredients: 3 (16 oz) pkgs vanilla wafers
1 (2 lbs) bag hot chocolate mix   ¼ cup hot water
10 (.75 oz) pkgs cream cheese
1 (3.5 oz) pkg vanilla whey drink
2 tbsps peanut butter

Directions: Crush vanilla wafers as fine as possible. Put half in one spread bowl and half in another spread bowl. Split hot chocolate mix in half and add to each bowl. Add 8 tbsps hot water to each bowl and knead well. Once both bowls are kneaded, put one bowl of mixture in a clean chip bag and flatten evenly. Cut open bag and put under a fan to dry for 3 to 4 hours. Repeat the procedure with second bowl. While this dries, combine the cream cheese, vanilla whey, peanut butter, and 3 tbsps hot water in an insert cup. Place cup in a hot pot so all melts. Stir occasionally. Once hot chocolate mixture is dry, spread cream mixture over the top of one piece but leave about 1 inch from edges all the way around. Put other piece on top. Cut and serve. If you are a baller, you can split a box of oatmeal cream pies in half using your ID card, and cream side facing down, decorate the top.

Min-choca Drops

Ingredients: 1 (16 oz) pkg Duplex cookies   1 (1 oz) mint stick
5 ½ tbsps hot water   ½ tsp coffee

Directions: Separate cream from cookies and set cream aside. Crush all cookies as fine as possible and put in a spread bowl. Crush mint stick and add to cookies. Add the 5 tbsps of hot water and the coffee to mixture and knead into a pliable dough. Divide mixture into pieces and roll into balls. Do not need to be big. Place cookie cream in an insert cup with a ½ tbsp of hot water and whip. Drizzle the icing over the product and place all on plain white paper to dry for 2 to 3 hours. Simply scrumptious.

Crunchy Chewy Granola

Ingredients: 5 tbsps hot chocolate mix   1 (2 oz) pkg trail mix
2 (43 grams) pkgs maple brown sugar oatmeal
2 tbsps peanut butter   3 tbsps cold water
2 (43 grams) pkgs regular oatmeal

Directions: In a spread bowl combine 2 tbsps hot chocolate mix with the rest of the ingredients. Mix all well, I mean well. Once mixed, divide mixture into 10 equal parts and roll into balls. Put the rest of the hot chocolate mix in a spread bowl and roll balls into mix to coat. Place them on plain white paper under a fan for 3 to 4 hours. Grab that coffee, you'll love em'.

Chocolate Covered Marshmallow Treats

Ingredients: 2 plain Hershey candy bars 1 tsp peanut butter
4 vanilla moon pies   1 (2 oz) bag salted peanuts

Directions: Cut up candy bars and put pieces and the peanut butter into an insert cup to melt thoroughly. While waiting, separate marshmallow from moon pies and put marshmallows in a spread bowl. Rinse the salt from the peanuts and lightly crush. After ingredients in the insert cup are fully melted, pour over the top of marshmallows and top with peanuts. Put this under a fan to dry for 3 hours.

Dirty Mudslide

Ingredients: 1 (16 oz) pkg Duplex cream cookies
2 vanilla moon pies
3 Milky Way candy bars   1 pkg nutty bars

2 tbsps peanut butter   ½ Butterfinger candy bar

Directions: Separate cream from cookies and set cream aside. Now, separate cookies by color. Crush chocolate ones as fine as possible. Add 2 tbsps of water to them and knead well. If too dry, add ½ tbsp of water and knead. Separate into three equally sized parts. Roll into a ball. The balls should be small enough to fit inside an insert cup. In this order, layer the insert cup: 1 chocolate cookie ball, marshmallow only from moon pie, 1 half diced Milky Way candy bar, 1 crushed nutty bar from package, and 1 tbsp of peanut butter. Repeat a second time and top with final chocolate ball and crushed Butterfinger candy bar. You will not use the vanilla parts of cookies or the cookie cream, nor will you use the cookie coating from moon pies. Place the insert cup in a hot pot to heat for 3 hours. OMG, you will not believe how good this is. Use all the leftovers to make a separate treat.

Oooie-Gooey & Chewy

Ingredients: 1 (8 oz) bag Bud's best Butterfinger cookies
                   10 (1 oz) chick-o-sticks   3 Milky Way candy bars

Directions: Crush all cookies and chick-o-sticks and put in a spread bowl. Cut all the candy bars into small pieces and place in an insert cup with 2 tbsps of hot water. Place in a hot pot to melt fully. Once all is melted, pour into the spread bowl and mix well. Two spoons are best for mixing. Cut open a clean chip bag and lay it on the bunk or desk. Using a spoon, separate this mixture into several pieces, roll into balls and flatten with spoon on bag. Put under a fan for 3 to 4 hours. Makes about 25 to 30 pieces. Enjoy!

Cereal Bars

Ingredients: 1 (20 oz) bag Frosted Mini Wheats cereal
¼ (2 lb) bag hot chocolate mix
1 box (10 pkg) instant oatmeal
¼ (10 oz) bag sunflower seeds
½ (18 oz) jar peanut butter   5 (2 oz) pkgs peanuts/trail mix
¼ cup hot water

Directions: You can use two spread bowls for this one or a clean cheese puffs bag. Crush all cereal, combine all the ingredients, and knead well. Make sure it is kneaded well. You do not want it off balanced. After you knead, use some cream cookie trays, and form the bars. Can fill trays to the top. Remove bars from trays by turning upside down and place all on plain, white paper. Put under a fan to dry for 8 hours. They are better to sit overnight. Does not sound like much, but they are very good.

Candy Bars

Ingredients: 3 (16 oz) pkgs cream cookies (any flavor)
1 (16 oz) bag vanilla wafers
6 (2 oz) pkgs salted peanuts   30 (1 oz) chick-o-sticks
1(2 lbs) bag hot chocolate mix
1 (10 oz) bag sunflower seeds
½ (18 oz) jar peanut butter   2 (12 oz) cherry Dr Peppers
You will need: a trash bag or 3 spread bowls

Directions: Separate cream from cookies and set the cream aside. Crush all cookies and wafers as fine as possible. Rinse the salt from the peanuts and crush up the chick-o-sticks. In a trash bag combine all ingredients and knead thoroughly. If you use spread bowls, divide all in thirds and knead thoroughly. Once kneaded, use the trays from cookies and form the bars. Remove bars from trays by turning upside down and place on plain, white paper. Dry under a fan for 8 hours. They are better to dry overnight. Once dry, put the cookie cream in an insert cup with 1 ½ tbsps water and stir well. Place this insert in a hot pot to melt for 1 hour. Pour over the top of the bars and dry for 2 hours. Awesome treat! You will love em'.

Baltimore's Best Bars

Ingredients: 2 (16 oz) pkgs cream cookies (any flavor)
10 (1 oz) chick-o-sticks   2 pkgs plain M&M's
1 box (10 pkg) instant oatmeal
3 (4 oz) servings raisins from tray
1 cup hot water   ½ (18 oz) jar peanut butter

Directions: Separate cream from cookies and set cream aside. Crush chick-o-sticks. Set M&M's aside for time being. In a large, clean, chip bag, combine all the rest of the ingredients, and knead well. The mixture will be very thick and stiff. Once kneaded, use cookie trays as a mold to form the bars. Fill the tray slots with mixture to the top. Remove the bars from the trays by turning tray upside down on plain, white paper and press in one corner. Bars will come loose this way. Put the bars under a fan for 8 hours. While they are drying, put the cream from the cookies in an insert cup with 1 tbsp hot water, stir well, then place in a hot pot to melt. When bars are dry, drizzle the icing over the top of the bars, lightly crush M&M's, and decorate the bars. Now allow them to dry under the fan for another 1 ½ hours.

Mint Chocolate Bars

Ingredients: 10 (1 oz) mint sticks
3 (3 oz) Ramen noodles (any flavor)
1 (2 lbs) bag hot chocolate mix
1 (12 oz) cherry Dr Pepper

Directions: Crush all mint sticks and place in an insert cup with 2 tbsps hot water. Stir well and place in a hot pot to melt fully. While it is melting, use a full hot sauce bottle to crush all the Ramen noodles. It is better to crush the noodles 1/3 at a time in the noodles bag. It takes a little time and work but make sure they are a fine powder when done. Place the powder in a spread bowl and add enough water to hydrate. Use a trash bag, which is better, to mix everything together or use 3 spread bowls. Split the noodle mixture and hot chocolate mix between the 3 bowls and knead together. Pour in the melted candy and mix again. Add 4 tbsps of Dr Pepper to each bowl and knead one last time. You do not want it too wet. Just past moist. If it gets too wet, add some oatmeal or crushed vanilla wafer. Get a couple of trays from cream cookies to mold all the bars. Fill trays about ¾ the way. Remove from trays and place on plain, white paper. Dry at least 8 hours but overnight is better.

Bighouse Bars

Ingredients: 1 (16 oz) bag vanilla wafers 1 box (10 pkgs) instant oatmeal
½ (18 oz) jar peanut butter   1 (10 oz) bag sunflower seeds
4 (2 oz) pkgs salted peanuts   3 pkgs plain M&M's

Directions: Crush vanilla wafers as fine as possible. Some chunks do not really matter. In a large clean chip bag or a large spread bowl combine all ingredients with ¼ cup cold water and knead thoroughly. You will need a couple trays from the cream cookies as molds to form bars. Once bars are formed, turn the trays upside down, remove bars on plain white paper and put under a fan for 4 to 6 hours. These are a great treat.

Fudge Cookies

Ingredients: 3 (16 oz) pkgs cream cookies (any flavor)
                        1 (2 lbs) bag hot chocolate mix
                        1 (16 oz) box oatmeal cream pies
                        2 (12 oz) Coca-Colas
You will need: thick, small trash bag or 3 large spread bowls

Directions: Separate the cream from all cookies and set cream aside. Crush cookies as fine as possible. If you have a trash bag, combine all the ingredients, except the cream, and knead the mixture very well. Take your time to make sure all is kneaded. Might need to add ½ can of water to this but really want it stiff. If you cannot get a trash bag, divide all the ingredients between the 3 spread bowls and knead separately. When done, roll all the mixture into balls, place each on plain, white paper and use a spoon to flatten into cookies. Let them sit under a fan to dry for 4 to 6 hours. Now, put the cream in an insert cup with 1 tbsp hot water. Stir well and place in hot pot to melt for about 1 hour. Drizzle it over the cookies and let sit for 1 ½ more hours. Heat up the coffee and invite a friend or two; you will have plenty.

Candy Oatmeal Cookies

Ingredients: 2 heaping tbsps peanut butter
                        1 Three Musketeers candy bar
                        3 (43 grams) pkgs regular oatmeal

3 (43 grams) pkgs maple brown sugar oatmeal
1 pkg plain M&M's   3 tbsps hot water

Directions: In a clean small chip bag combine peanut butter and the Three Musketeers. Place in a hot pot so that all can fully melt. While waiting, in a spread bowl combine all the oatmeal, M&M's, and hot water. After ingredients melt, pour into the spread bowl, mix, and knead well. Once kneaded, separate mixture into 10 to 12 pieces and roll into a ball. On clean, white paper place balls and use a spoon to flatten into a cookie. Let them sit under a fan to dry for 2 to 3 hours. When ready, heat up your coffee. Eat and drink up.

Chocolate Oatmeal Cookies

Ingredients: 4 tbsps butter   10 pkgs sweeteners
                    ½ cup instant milk   1/3 cup hot chocolate mix
                    1 box (10 pkgs) instant oatmeal   ½ cup peanut butter

Directions: Use a clean chip bag and combine butter, sweeteners, instant milk, and hot chocolate mix. Place in a hot pot and fully melt. The hotter the pot, the better. Heat for about 3 hours. Add no water, the butter will be the liquid. In a spread bowl mix all oatmeal together. When mixture in pot is fully melted, stir in peanut butter until all is smooth. This mixture will be really thick. Pour mixture into oatmeal and stir well. If the oatmeal is flavored, you will not need all 10 sweeteners. You can use 5. Once all is mixed, divide mixture into 10 to 12 equal parts. Roll each into a ball. Place balls on plain white paper and use a spoon to flatten into a cookie. Put them under a fan for 3 to 4 hours. MMM! Mix up the coffee, it's time to eat!

Chocolate Drop Sugar Cookies

Ingredients: 2 (16 oz) pkgs vanilla wafers
                    12 pkgs sweetener (regular sugar if available)
                    ¼ cup hot water
                    ½ (3 oz) Ramen noodles (no seasoning)
                    ¼ (2 lb) bag hot chocolate mix   1 (12 oz) Coca-Cola

Directions: Crush all vanilla wafers as fine as possible and put in a spread bowl. Add all sweeteners and hot water and knead into a thick, pliable dough. Crush noodles, using a full hot sauce bottle, into a super fine powder. Better to crush 1/3 at a time, so it is a fine powder. Combine noodles, hot chocolate mix, and about ¼ of the soda (a little less than ½ cup) and knead well. Divide wafer mixture into pieces and roll into balls. Do not want too big. Use your palm to smash cookies just a bit, but leave thick. Use your thumb and press in the center of cookies to create a dent. Carefully take some of the chocolate mix, roll into small balls and put inside the dent. Press firmly on cookies. Place them on plain, white paper and put under a fan for 3 to 4 hours. It takes a little time; however, your creativity will be well appreciated.

Peanut Butter Cookies

Ingredients: 1 (13 oz) box graham crackers
2 (2 oz) pkgs salted peanuts
½ (18 oz) jar peanut butter
3 (43 grams) pkgs maple brown sugar oatmeal

Directions: In a spread bowl crush the graham crackers. Rinse the salt from the peanuts. Combine all the ingredients in the spread bowl, add 2 tbsps of hot water, and knead well. Divide mixture into 10 to 12 equal parts and roll into balls. Place them on plain, white paper and use a spoon to flatten into a cookie. Put under a fan to dry for 4 to 6 hours. Once again, heat up coffee and enjoy.

Puddings

Banana Pudding

Ingredients: 3 banana moon pies   1 heaping tbsp butter
1 (16 oz) bag vanilla wafers
1 (2 oz) energy mix (optional)

Directions: Crush the moon pies and cut up marshmallow. Combine moon pies and butter in an insert cup and place in a hot pot to melt. In a spread bowl layer with vanilla wafers and pour moon pie mixture over top. Repeat this process until all mixture is gone. If you use energy mix, sprinkle between layers. Once done, let sit for 30 minutes.

Lemon Pudding

Ingredients: 1 (16 oz) bag vanilla wafers   1 pkg sweetener
1 (12 oz) Sprite
1 (.34 oz) pkg lemon lime sports drink mix
1 (3.2 oz) pkg instant milk

Directions: Crush half the bag of vanilla wafers as fine as possible. Set other half aside. In a large spread bowl combine crushed wafers, sweetener, ¾ (1 ¼ cups) Sprite, lemon lime sports drink mix, and instant milk. Whip the mixture well. Once all is mixed, layer a separate spread bowl with vanilla wafers and pour the mixture over top. Repeat this until all is gone. Put under a fan for 2 hours.

Chocolate Pudding

Ingredients: 3 chocolate moon pies   1 Milky Way
                2 tbsps butter   1 (16 oz) bag vanilla wafers
                1 (2 oz) bag salted peanuts (optional)

Directions: Separate marshmallow from moon pies. Crush cookie part and cut marshmallow parts and Milky Way into pieces. Combine these items and the butter in an insert cup and place in a hot pot to heat. The hotter the pot, the better. Once all is melted, layer a spread bowl with vanilla wafers and pour mixture over top. Repeat this process until all the mixture is gone. Once complete, put under a fan for 2 hours. If you use the peanuts, rinse them well and top off pudding with them. MMMMMM Good!

Another Chocolate Pudding

Ingredients: 1 (16 oz) pkg double fudge or chocolate cream cookies
                1 cup hot chocolate mix   2 pkgs sweetener
                1 (3.2 oz) pkg instant milk   1 (12 oz) Coca-Cola

Directions: Separate the cream from the cookies and set cookies aside. In a large spread bowl combine hot chocolate mix, sweeteners, cookie cream, instant milk, and about ¾ can of Coke (1 ¼ cups). Whip this mixture well. Use two spoons. You do not want any lumps. Once smooth and creamy, pour the mixture into a large clean chip bag. Place it in a hot pot to heat for 2 hours. When mixture is ready, layer bowl with a row of cookies. Top cookies with mixture. Repeat this process until all is gone. Put it under a fan for 3 hours. Just like home. Enjoy.

Butterfinger Delight Fudge

Ingredients: ¼ cup (about 30) crushed vanilla wafers
                1 (43 grams) pkg regular oatmeal   2 tbsps hot chocolate mix
                2 tbsps instant milk   1 (3.5 oz) pkg vanilla whey
                4 tbsps chocolate syrup   3 macaroon cookies
                1 Butterfinger

Directions: Put crushed vanilla wafers in a spread bowl. Add the
oatmeal, hot chocolate mix, and 1 tbsp hot water and knead well. In a
separate bowl combine instant milk, vanilla whey, chocolate syrup, and 2
tbsps hot water and mix well. Crush the macaroon cookies and mix in milk
mixture. Mix both bowls together and knead into a dough. Place mixture
into a clean chip bag and flatten like a pizza. Cut open bag, crush
Butterfinger, and sprinkle on top. Now put it under a fan to dry for 4 hours.
Cut and serve. This is greatttt!!!

Baltimore's Fabulous Fudge

Ingredients: 4 (3 oz) Ramen noodles (any flavor)
                2 (16 oz) pkgs vanilla/Duplex cream cookies
                1 (12 oz) Coca Cola   15 (1 oz) chick-o-sticks (crushed)
                6 oatmeal cream pies   1 ½ cups oatmeal (any flavor)
                1 (2 lbs) bag hot chocolate mix
                4 (2 oz) pkgs salted peanuts
                1 ½ tbsps plantation blend coffee   hot water
You will need: a thick trash bag or 3 spread bowls

Directions: Crush Ramen noodles into a fine powder. Better to crush 1/3 at a time by using a full hot sauce bottle. Takes awhile and some work. Now, separate the cream from the cookies and set cream aside. If you have a trash bag, combine all ingredients except the cream filling, coffee, and hot water. Now, add one cup of hot water and knead very well. Will be very thick and stiff. Flatten mixture in bag* and shape into a large square. Cut trash bag open and dry under a fan overnight.

While fudge is drying, make the icing. Place cookie cream and coffee in an insert cup with 1tbsp hot water and mix. Place insert cup in a hot pot to heat for 1 hour. Once melted, either drizzle over bars or pour on fudge and spread. Let the fudge and icing sit overnight. Once done, cut and serve. Just as the recipe states, these are fabulous!!

*If you use the spread bowls, divide ingredients into thirds in bowls and knead each one thoroughly. Use the trays from the cookies and mold mixture in the trays to form bars. Dry under a fan overnight. After you form bars, remove them from trays by turning upside down on plain white paper.

Ingredient Conversion Table

Packaged Meat

Beef Stew --11.25 oz pkg
Beef Tips in Gravy --------------------------8 oz pkg
Chicken chili ------------------------------------11.25 oz pkg
Chicken chunks -----------------------------7 oz pkg
Chili with/without beans---------------------11.25 oz pkg
Mackerel ---3.5 oz pkg
Mexican Beef ----------------------------------8 oz pkg
Pepperoni Slices ------------------------------3.5 oz pkg
Pot Roast---11.25 oz pkg
Sardine --3.53 oz pkg
Shredded Beef in BBQ sauce ----------------11.25 oz pkg
Spam --3 oz pkg
Summer Sausage------------------------------5 oz pkg
Tuna --4.23 oz pkg
Tomato Basil soup mix ----------------------15 oz pkg

Drinks

Electrolyte/Sports Drink mix-----------------1 single pkg (.34 oz) or 1 tsp
Hot Chocolate mix----------------------------2 lb bag
Instant Cappuccino ---------------------------.81 oz pkg
Instant Coffee --------------------------------4 oz bag
Instant Milk-----------------------------------3.2 oz bag
Instant Tea -----------------------------------100 count box
Juices/soda------------------------------------12 oz cans
Whey/Chike -----------------------------------3.5 oz pkg

Cookies

Vanilla, Strawberry, Duplex, Peanut Butter, Fudge
Cream cookies:-------------------------------16 oz pkg
Bud's Best-------------------------------------8 oz pkg
Chocolate Chip, Oatmeal, Macaroon -------12 oz pkg
Graham Crackers ----------------------------13 oz box

Maria Cookies ----------------------------------- 5.6 oz pkg
Regal Graham ----------------------------------- 8 oz box
Vanilla Wafers ---------------------------------- 16 oz bag

Candy/Pastries

Butterscotch ------------------------------------ 7.5 oz bag
Candy bars-------------------------------------- regular size
Chick-O-Sticks--------------------------------- 1 oz single
Fireballs--- 6 oz bag
Fruit Disc -------------------------------------- 8 oz bag
Mint/Fruit Sticks------------------------------- 1 oz single
Orange Slices----------------------------------- 10.25 oz bag
Pastries --- reg size single
Pie (lemon, cherry) --------------------------- 4 oz (4" x 2" box)

Chips/Crackers

BBQ Chips ------------------------------------- 8 oz bag
Cheese Nips ------------------------------------ 18 oz box
Cheese Puffs----------------------------------- 10 oz bag
Cheetos--- 3 oz bag
Corn Chips-------------------------------------- 16 oz bag
Hot Fries --------------------------------------- 1.25 oz bag
Jalapeno Chips --------------------------------- 8 oz bag
Nacho Chips------------------------------------ 3 oz bag
Packaged Crackers, Cheese & Chive, etc.-- 1.375 oz pkg
Party Mix -------------------------------------- 11 oz bag
Pork Skins -------------------------------------- 1.75 oz bag
Regular Potato Chips-------------------------- 8 oz bag
Salsa Verde Chips ------------------------------ 6 oz bag
Saltine Crackers-------------------------------- box 4 sleeves
Tortilla Chips----------------------------------- 16 oz bag

Little Debbies

Chocolate Covered Peanuts ------------------- 8 oz bag
Cup Cakes -------------------------------------- 11 oz pkg
Donut Sticks------------------------------------ 10 oz box

Malt Balls--------------------------------------3 oz bag
Moon Pies --------------------------------------2.75 oz singles
Nutty Bars -------------------------------------12 oz box
Oatmeal Cream Pies--------------------------16 oz box
Rice Crispy Treats----------------------------4.75 oz box
Swiss Rolls -------------------------------------13 oz box

Misc

Beef & Cheese Sticks --------------------------average size pack
Cereal ---20 oz bag
Chocolate Syrup ------------------------------16 oz bottle
Corn nuts--------------------------------------6 oz bag
Cup --12 oz coffee cup
Energy/Trail mix------------------------------2 oz bag
Flour Tortilla ----------------------------------27.2 oz 12 pack
Hot/Salted/Un-Salted Peanuts --------------2 oz bag
Instant Oatmeal --------------------------------10 pkg box (43 gram pkgs)
Instant Potatoes -------------------------------4 oz bag
Instant Rice-------------------------------------8 oz bag
Ramen Noodles --------------------------------3 oz pkg
Refried Beans ----------------------------------12 oz bag
Sunflower Seeds -------------------------------10 oz bag
Tray Servings-Fruit---------------------------4 oz
Tray Servings-Meat --------------------------8 oz
Tray Servings-Veggies-----------------------4 oz

Condiments

BBQ Sauce --------------------------------------18 oz bottle
Chili Con Queso -------------------------------15 oz bottle
Cream Cheese----------------------------------.75 oz single
Garlic Powder----------------------------------3 oz bottle
Habanero/Hot Sauce --------------------------5 oz bottle
Jalapeno Pepper--------------------------------singles 1.3 oz
Jelly-Grape -------------------------------------12 oz bottle
Ketchup ---13.5 oz bottle
Mustard ---16 oz bottle
Onion Flakes -----------------------------------3 oz bottle

Onion Powder ----------------------------------- 3 oz bottle
Peanut Butter (creamy)------------------------ 18 oz jar
Picante Sauce---------------------------------- 12 oz bottle
Pickle--- single 9 oz pkg
Ranch Dressing ------------------------------- 1.5 oz pkg
Relish--- 8 oz bottle
Salad Dressing ------------------------------- 14 oz bottle
Salsa-- 12 oz bottle
Sandwich Spread ----------------------------- 14 oz bottle
Seasoning Packet ----------------------------- single, from Ramen Noodle
Soy Sauce-------------------------------------- 5 oz bottle or home made
Spice-Coriander & Annatto ------------------ 1.5 oz bag
Squeeze Cheese ------------------------------- 16 oz bottle
Strawberry Preserves------------------------- 12 oz bottle
Sweetener-------------------------------------- 100 count box = 2 tsp sugar

Made in the USA
Monee, IL
02 October 2022

15001220R00072